Beyond Neoliberalism

Beyond Neoliberalism

Alain Touraine

Translated by David Macey

Polity

First published in France as *Comment sortir du libéralisme?* © Librairie
Arthème Fayard, 1998.

Published with the assistance of the French Ministry of Culture.

First published in 2001 by Polity Press in association with Blackwell
Publishers Ltd.

Editorial office:
Polity Press
65 Bridge Street
Cambridge CB2 1UR, UK

Marketing and production:
Blackwell Publishers Ltd
108 Cowley Road
Oxford OX4 1JF, UK

Published in the USA by
Blackwell Publishers Inc.
350 Main Street
Malden, MA 02148, USA

ISBN 0–7456–2433–2
ISBN 0–7456–2434–0 (pbk)

A catalogue record for this book is available from the British Library and
has been applied for from the Library of Congress.

Typeset in 11 on 13 pt Berling
by Ace Filmsetting Ltd, Frome, Somerset
Printed in Great Britain by MPG Books Ltd, Bodmin, Cornwall

This book is printed on acid-free paper.

Contents

Introduction   1

1   The return of capitalism   8

2   Four exits   24

3   New social movements?   45

4   The social left and the ultra-left   74

5   Two possible policies: the third way and a
    two-and-a-half policy   89

Conclusions   106

Notes   118

Index   120

tors have been plunged. Its answer to liberal policies is, or seems to be, state interventionism, but it rarely makes concrete proposals.

The third mode of critique, which is the inspiration behind this book, is opposed to all those representations that deny the possibility of positive action. On the contrary, it asserts that new actors are appearing and that they are demanding rights and identities. It also holds that the demand for cultural rights is now the factor that will allow new actors to appear and that this is the one demand that can restore a capacity for action that has been sapped for the last twenty years, largely because the forces of resistance and opposition are drowning in the attempt to defend an economic model that has long been inadequate and whose effects are becoming more and more perverse.

This allows us to analyse a situation, define possible actors and even suggest what might become a new social policy.

If, however, we are to understand the nature and possibility of collective action, we must first get rid of the invasive theme of globalization, which acts on us like a drug. Globalization is a purely ideological representation or an expression of the despair and anxiety of those who are indeed the victims of new technologies, industrial concentration, financial gambles and the relocation of certain activities in the new industrial countries. We must break out of this vicious circle and, in order to do so, we must begin with analysis. Although we are being submerged by discourses on globalization, we are not being given any concrete proof of our social and political impotence in the face of what has to be called by its real name: a capitalist offensive. There are in fact no grounds for asserting that, all at once, social policies have become impossible, that industrial policies have only negative effects, that technology serves only the interests of the dominant financial interests, and that the collapse of the old administrative ways of managing the economy can only lead to the triumph of deregulated markets. This approach implies that we must make alliances with those who point to the weaknesses and failures of the administered economy, which does not even have the egalitarian effects some ascribe to it. Yes, we have to abandon the administered economy completely, both because it is economically destructive and because the opening up of world markets allows, or even demands, both new social policies and a quest for participation and justice.

So let us stop all this prophesying and this repeating of the litany of *la pensée unique*, whose central argument, shared by enemies and supporters alike, is that the globalization of the economy leaves nation-states and social movements impotent. Let us look, rather, at reality in the light of the following three propositions:

(1) Globalization is no more than a set of tendencies. They are all important, but there is little connection between them. The assertion that an essentially liberal world society is being created and that it is impervious to national political interventions, is purely ideological.

(2) Even the most justified of protests may lead us into a blind alley if those who voice them do not believe in the collective possibility of transforming society and establishing new forms of social controls on the economy.

(3) This work of reconstruction presupposes that social action and political interventions complement one another, even though there will be tensions and conflicts between the two. Throughout this analysis, I will be referring to the contemporary social situation and contemporary collective actions so as to demonstrate that they have at least two meanings. On the one hand, we have despairing denunciations of the contradictions of the capitalist system, which can lead only to marginal revolts or reliance upon authoritarian power; on the other, we have the desire to help victims transform themselves into actors. As the first meaning tends to become dominant, the second obviously tends to fade. That is why our analysis must be a critique not of what we call the movement of society, but of the most alienating interpretations that have been made of it and that are so readily accepted in a country which, for twenty years, has indeed been aware that it is living through a crisis, and that its social situation will inevitably worsen under the impact of the blows inflicted on it by world markets.

We must, finally, recognize that intellectuals have a particular responsibility. They, more so than any other category, must see to it that protests do not degenerate into pointless denunciations and that they do, on the contrary, lead to the formation of new social actors and, indirectly, new economic and social policies.

This critical analysis would, however, lead nowhere if political power were to remain indifferent to social struggles, be suspicious of them and be content to adopt a centrist policy of combining a neoliberal management of the economy with a single-minded concern with public order and security. If the ruling majority does not feel that it has a duty to represent the most unprivileged sectors of society, why be surprised when those sectors allow themselves to be seduced by the prophets of breakdown and catastrophe?

Almost the whole of Western Europe is governed by centre-left parties or coalitions. But those governments still seem to be hesitating between centrist policies which are increasingly sensitive to the interest of a vast middle class that has to be defended and reassured, and a policy of actively fighting social exclusion. Some think it advantageous to increase the distance, in both words and deeds, that divorces social struggles from political programmes. I, in contrast, would like to see governments giving their programmes a greater social content. Ultimately, this book is an attempt to defend both independent social movements and more active policies in the fight against exclusion.

1
The return of capitalism

In order to understand political struggles, economic difficulties and intellectual debates, we must be able to define the historical situation in which they develop.

Some speak to us only of the economy. If their point of view is correct, political life has no meaning and power should, as a matter of urgency, be handed over to the governor of the Central Bank. Others make a better claim on our attention by stressing the rapid growth of an information society that is spreading across the world and transforming all our activities. They are right to say that we leaving industrial society behind and that what, thirty years ago, I was calling post-industrial society should in fact be called the information society.[1] In this new society, social actors, social issues and social relations are being transformed, and have already undergone profound transformations. We found it so difficult to understand, in the nineteenth century, that we had entered industrial society and were no longer living in Balzac's France that we are now more careful not to be one society behind the times. We are well aware that, important as they may be, conflicts of interest between employers and industrial workers are no longer central to social and political life and that the words 'communism' and 'socialism' either no longer mean anything or mean something different from what they meant at the beginning of the last century. The sociological or historical analysis of the world in which we live obliges us to recognize that we have moved from one mode of production, social relations and self-representations to another, and not only from industrial society to the dissolution of all societies into those markets that are described as either heaven or hell. But, pertinent as they may be, it is not in these terms that we have to define the situation in which we live today.

The collective actions which, over twenty years ago, I described as new social movements – like the May '68 movement itself – gave birth to new actors and new ideas that foreshadowed the new society that was being established. Those movements have now been greatly weakened, when they still exist. What is of concern on the social and political stage is no longer how knowledge is being used in research, or health care, or the media, but unemployment, growing inequality, exclusion and, to move away from everyday life, the widespread awareness that we are impotent in the face of economic forces that are more powerful than states. We are particularly worried by what some call the end of the nation-state. What we are living through is therefore not so much a change of society as a change in the mode of modernization. The difference of registers is easily explained. To speak of industrial society or the information society is to speak of a type of society; when, on the other hand, we say that we are moving from a state-controlled administered economy to a market economy, we are talking about a change in the mode of modernization. I would immediately add, at risk of surprising some readers, that capitalism and socialism are modes of modernization and not types of society. The defining feature of capitalism is that change is managed by the market; that of socialism is the dominant role played by the state. We might add that the state that controls historical change can be either national or foreign, just as markets may be local, national or international. We can therefore say, as a first approximation, that *we have moved from a form of socialism to a form of capitalism*, and that *the market has replaced the state as the principal regulatory force in our society*. Many define this transformation simply as the deregulation of a market which was previously held prisoner by bureaucrats and politicians. That judgement cannot be defended. Why use the expression *les trente glorieuses* (the 'thirty glorious years' between 1945 and 1975) to describe a period when the state had a strong hold over the economy and society, if that hold was always destructive? The great technocrats who, like Bloch-Lainé, Gruson, Delouvrier, Massé and so many others, presided over the reconstruction and modernization of the French economy had – did they not? – a global vision of French society, and they were just as concerned with social justice as with the pursuit of economic efficiency.

They did indeed have a global vision. After the war, most countries in the world had integrated projects for national development in which economic, social and national objectives were all linked. This mode of development was victorious throughout the world. It triumphed both in Europe, where the wartime ruins had to be rebuilt, and in Latin America, where economists who were as concerned with social advances as they were with growth relied upon 'national popular' states to launch a programme of 'inward' development. Elsewhere, the main objective of countries emerging from decolonization was to build new nations. The communist countries, finally, adopted non-democratic versions of these integrated projects for national development.

This integrated and global mode of development was gradually exhausted and, from the 1970s onwards, it was overthrown by a different mode which gave priority to the market. In many cases, national and state-administered development had resulted in a poor allocation of resources and, sometimes, bureaucratization and corruption. The competitiveness of many sectors had been weakened. At the same time, the goal of reducing social equalities was achieved less and less often, as early left-wing criticisms of the welfare state in Great Britain and France demonstrated. In symbolic terms, the oil crises marked the beginning of a new era: the money levied on the industrial countries by the oil-producing countries was invested in American banks which were looking for borrowers all over the world, and especially in Latin America. The economy was being globalized. At the same time, states like Japan and Korea were prioritizing exports and thus became new industrial countries which represented a formidable competitive threat to the old industrialized countries. There was, especially in our countries, a feeling that it was now necessary to free the economy from rules and controls that could no longer be justified in the name of reducing inequalities and which were leading to spectacular crashes, especially in France where the collapse of public sector companies like Crédit Lyonnais, Air France, GAN and GIAT cost us dearly. For twenty years, most of the national debate has therefore been largely pre-occupied with the critique of the 'French exception', the economic failures of the public sector, the weight of the bureaucracy, elitist patterns of recruitment into the ruling classes and many other themes. Many of these criticisms are well founded.

But justifiable and indispensable as these criticisms are, there is a danger that they will make us miss the essential point. The idea that an economy can be freed from all social and political controls is absurd. The economy is a system of means that must be made to serve political ends. To say that 'the economy has to be freed from clumsy state intervention and modes of social management that have become inefficient' is one thing; to say that 'markets must be self-regulating and free from all external intervention' is quite another.

There is a name for this second way of thinking: capitalism. This is by no means the same thing as the globalization of the economy, which, despite all the talk we hear of it, remains remarkably ill-defined. Capitalism is a market economy to the extent that it rejects all external controls and tries, on the contrary, to act on the whole of society as it pursues its own interests. Capitalism is a society that is dominated by its economy. Hence the danger inherent in the current destruction of the old mode of managing the economy; its destruction is both indispensable and dangerous because what is at stake is the transition from one way of placing social controls on the economy to another without surrendering to the illusion that all social controls on the economy can be removed. That illusion leads to growing inequalities and all kinds of marginalization and exclusion.

These comments are, truth to tell, too moderate. Think of the effects of the triumph of capitalism at the end of the nineteenth century and the beginning of the twentieth. As an increasingly finance-based capitalism became hegemonic, nations that were losing control of their economies flung themselves into a nationalism which could take either a revolutionary or a reactionary form. No matter which form it took, this nationalism led to the break-up of the industrial world, to all the revolutions that occurred before and during the First World War and to the establishment of totalitarian regimes. The economy had tried to dominate society and politics; politics now came to dominate both the economy and society. In both cases, social life, commerce, participation and therefore democracy were the main victims of the upheaval. If we now allow ourselves to be ruled by the interests of finance capitalism, we can look forward to a twenty-first century that will be even more violent and war-torn than the twentieth.

These observations may find an audience, but I know they will have difficulty in convincing anyone. We are inundated by a ubiquitous discourse that comes to us from left and right alike, from international organizations and from wage-earners whose companies have decided to relocate: given that we live in a globalized society consisting of transformations and technologies, of new transnational units of production and financial networks, and given that new industrial countries where wages are often very low are entering it too, it is absurd to speak of political choice; we really have no choice but to adapt as best we can to the new conditions of international economic life. It is true that the United States has a lot of room for manoeuvre but this is because globalization usually means Americanization, and because the United States enjoys a hegemonic position in both cultural and military terms. Is there any need to repeat yet again what we hear every day? What has just been said is enough to explain our feeling of impotence and, therefore, the echo of the discourses that denounce this development, condemn the Maastricht and Amsterdam treaties and demand the defence and reconstruction of the nation-state.

And what if it were all untrue? What if it were nothing more than an ideological bubble that bursts when we prick it with an analysis?

We must first, as I have already pointed out, make a distinction between the information society and the globalized economy. The real-time availability of information is an important phenomenon, but no one has ever claimed that the telegraph or even the development of the electrical industry explained either the state of the economy in 1900 or Great Britain's supremacy. Robert Reich and Manuel Castells paint a much more accurate picture when they demonstrate that companies are becoming mediators between the world of markets and the world of technologies. And in doing so they demolish with a single blow half the ideological construct I am criticizing. The United States enjoys its current supremacy mainly because it invented and developed new technologies that Germany or France have been slow to master, and because it has modified the forms of organization and authority that are bound up with those new technologies. European countries remain too attached to the old industrial model that says 'big is beautiful.' All this is very important and it identifies one of the main fields where our future will be decided, but it has little to do with globalization.

It is true that transnational companies are asserting themselves and that they are increasingly organized into networks; it is also true that international commerce is growing faster than world output. But wasn't this also true twenty or thirty years ago, at a time when catastrophic talk of globalization was almost unknown? We simply have to recognize, like every sociologist since Durkheim – who was writing one hundred years ago – that the density of trade increases as modernity progresses and that the fact that it increases is one of the best definitions of modernity, even if the acceleration of that phenomenon does constantly modify social life and especially the international economy. In the space of a few decades, we have seen countries escaping from poverty and we have seen hundreds of millions of new consumers and producers rendering obsolete the antiquated distinction between the developed world and the third world. A large part of the third world is 'emerging' at the very time when a sizeable fraction of the developed world is being submerged.

If we turn to the development of financial networks, the

extraordinary thing is that the international trade in goods and services represents only a minute proportion of the capital in circulation. It is true that capital can change hands and pass through different bank accounts several times a day, and it is in fact this that makes the dominance of what, in 1910, Rudolf Hilferding was already calling finance capitalism so obvious. The phenomenon is not necessarily bound up with technological change and the internationalization of markets. In France, we have recently lived through a period in which consumer spending was low, and in which economic policies were often incoherent or contradictory. During that period capital had a greater share than labour in the gross national product. Productive investment rose more slowly than investment in the financial markets, which were sometimes very volatile. International public opinion saw them as so many tornadoes that brought ruin and poverty. What gives us the idea that this hyperdevelopment of finance capital is unavoidable? It might also be argued that the reappearance of some growth in Europe will lead to more productive investment, that migrant capital will be contained by new controls and will stabilize, especially in the industrial countries to which it is attracted by technological developments and, it is to be hoped, a revival of the spirit of enterprise.

It has to be said that the main cause of the threats that hang over us is neither the globalization of the economy nor the emergence of new industrial countries, but capital's freedom to move around the world. The best proof of this is that those countries that have taken measures to restrict its movement, like Chile, which does have a free market economy, and China, which has a very different economic system, have been protected from the crisis that has hit Mexico, Indonesia and so many other countries. Free trade in goods and the unrestricted movement of capital are two very different things. Joseph Stiglitz, who is the World Bank's chief economist, and the MIT economist Paul Krugman are convinced supporters of economic neo-liberalism, but they both think that nation-states should control the movement of capital. So let us stop blaming every aspect of the economy, from new technologies to the new international division of labour, and look at where the danger really lies: in the unrestricted movement of capital, which can suddenly destroy whole economies on the basis of a purely financial and short-term calculation. The responsibility for such catastrophes is shared between international capital and states which cannot (or will not) defend their economies, or which are brought down because their own financial systems are out of balance.

The bursting of the financial bubble in Japan in the 1990s, the disastrous effects of the excessive debts contracted by big economic groups in Korea and the political weakness of the Indonesian government demonstrated in dramatic fashion that economy, finance and politics are not a monolithic bloc. They can be combined in many different ways, some ruinous and some useful. Corruption, the absence of any policy on wealth redistribution and the economic irresponsibility of many financial groups are all factors that lead to a crisis.

The crisis that threatens to destroy both the economy and political power in Russia should cure us once and for all of the idea that the globalization of the economy and the internationalization of financial circuits are such powerful phenomena that no political intervention can control them. How can we fail to see that this is primarily a political crisis? Whereas the former communist countries of Central Europe did construct market economies, and at times put former communists back in power, Russia's attempts at reconversion were unsuccessful because Boris Yeltsin made a complete break with the communist system in 1991. There was no longer an efficient public administration because the state was incapable of collecting taxes and had no clear programme of action. In their absence, Russia reverted to a kind of primitive economy based upon the export of raw materials and the investment of most capital abroad. The Russian crisis has had an effect on world capitalism, but it cannot be said that it was the penetration of capital in itself that triggered the crisis. Most of the blame obviously lies with the authorities, who were incapable of establishing the conditions for growth and stability. We therefore have to stress the extreme danger created by the mobility of capital that is in search of financial profits rather than productive investments, admit that this is only one aspect of the crisis, and recognize that governments are largely to blame.

Does it have to be stressed, finally, that another major aspect of globalization – namely the American hegemony that has been so visible since 1989 – does not entirely stem from the globalization of the economy, since it is the logical outcome of the United States's victory in the cold war against the Soviet empire? There are no grounds for believing that the United States could always force a new Gulf War on its allies. The only thing that prevents Europe from playing a leading international role is its political and diplomatic weakness.

So let us stop denouncing globalization and neoliberalism in the same breath. We should be blaming finance capitalism and we should remember that, as Élie Cohen in particular has reminded us, the state still has a great capacity to intervene in most sectors of national life, and that economic logic is not implacable.

The coming into force of the Maastricht and Amsterdam treaties may even lend a new importance to European countries' policies for technological development and to their social policies. Our states can no longer use their traditional budgetary or monetary instruments to implement their policies, and they will soon lose control of their fiscal instruments too. Political life will no longer resound with endless and repetitive statements about the importance of a balanced budget or the strong franc and the weak lira. We will be obliged – fortunately – to start talking once more about production, the redistribution of the product of collective labour, the avoidance of major risks, better education and health care, ways of improving the social welfare system and providing decent retirement pensions, the need to rebuild our cities, and the management of an increasingly multicultural society.

After these commonsense remarks, what remains of the idea of globalization? Nothing. It really is nothing more than ideological scaremongering. It is an attempt to convince us that a new global unity has been built on the ruins of the integrated national development projects of the postwar period, and that it is at once economic, social and international. They would have us believe that we have gone from a statist society to a neoliberal society, and that the planned economy has been replaced by the market economy. I hope that I have said enough to convince my readers that reality is the very opposite to what this ideology asserts it to be. *We have in reality moved from integrated national models to an international situation in which the various dimensions of economic, social and cultural life have become separated and divorced from one another.*

Then why has *la pensée unique* been so successful? The dominant economic and financial milieus certainly have a lot to do with it: a certain number of books, of very variable quality, have succeeded in vaunting the superiority of neoliberal economic policies. But it is difficult to understand why this propaganda should have been so successful at a time when unemployment is rising and discontent is growing.

The idea of globalization has in fact been popularized by the ultra-left rather than the right. The ultra-left tries to justify the preservation of the traditional forms of the administered economy on the grounds that it is impossible to create new forms of social controls on the economy. The opening up of the economy to world markets and the defence of vested social interests proved to be a good combination, as they both led to the marginalization and sometimes even the exclusion of less well protected categories. The weakness of trade union action and, especially in France, its almost complete identification with the defence of public sector jobs finally left the field clear for the economic and financial actors who are trying to convince us that the only remaining obstacle to the exercise of their freedom is the protection of vested interests and that it is the weakest categories who bear the brunt of the negative economic effects of that protection. In other words, it is not so much the economic as the social situation that has encouraged the mass diffusion of a capitalist ideology which suits both right- and left-wing social conservatives, as well as the golden boys of the financial world.

This should, it might be said in passing, encourage us to act in such a way as to transform social relations. French trade unionism has been collapsing for twenty years and the union federations have lost between one-third and two-thirds of their members. Although they have been weakened to some extent, trade unions remain powerful in Germany, Sweden and Italy, and their strength has allowed Italy to pursue a successful policy of both economic liberalization and equilibrium with the support of both the main party of the left and the big unions. Italy provides a remarkable example – almost as remarkable as Denmark, the Netherlands and Portugal – of how it is possible to reconcile economic neoliberalism with social welfare. French public opinion continues to regard the two as incompatible. As a result, our country has gone from Charybdis to Scylla. The result is discontent and fear.

It is obviously legitimate to speak of the globalization of the economy. But that does not necessarily mean that we can say that a new integrated model is taking shape. We are in fact witnessing the very opposite of that: a growing divorce between the economic system (and especially the financial economy) and the social whole to which it should belong. The social, cultural and political reaction to this is increasingly identity-based, or based upon interests that are no longer economic but sustained by a self-consciousness, which can be ethnic, national or religious. The world is not becoming unified; it is fragmenting. In that sense, Huntington is right and Fukuyama is wrong, but Huntington's books are no more convincing than Fukuyama's. The idea that one social model is accepted (if not respected) throughout the world, and that it is a combination of a market economy, representative democracy and cultural tolerance, is obviously wrong. In many parts of the world, fundamentalisms of all kinds are triumphant. The United States has been particularly affected by 'identity politics', which destroys citizenship and therefore the capacity for political action, especially at a time when political parties are increasingly being influenced by financial lobbies.

The effect of this dissociation has been to produce two contrasting discourses: that of economic globalization, and that of cultural identity. Their appearance is both a cause and an effect of the destruction of systems of state intervention and of truly political debate, and of a lack of direction on the part of the social sciences. Given the political void that exists between the internationalized economy and the defence of increasingly particular identities, it is impossible for social movements capable of transforming their country's politics to emerge. This explains the scale of the revolts and, in some countries, the violence. Those who make a virtue out of necessity and stress the anti-institutional or purely critical aspect of collective action, are helping to close the vicious circle in which objective situations and subjective reactions – individual and collective – reinforce one another. This makes political action impossible. It lessens, that is, a country's ability to act upon itself in such a way as to reduce the dangerous divorce between the economy and cultures.

This critical analysis of the idea of globalization leads us to two conclusions. The first is of a historical nature. There is no more reason to believe in the formation of a world society than there was on the eve of the First World War in 1913. Like most ideologies, the idea of globalization has come to dominate the public scene at the very moment when it ceases to be of any real analytic use or, more specifically, at the moment when in many countries, including France, there is once more talk of production and state intervention, as well as of equality and social welfare.

The second concerns us more directly. If the idea of globalization, which aspires to being the foundation myth of the world capitalist society, is no more than an ideological construct, we will, when we shatter it, rediscover an awareness of our ability to act, of our responsibilities and of the pertinence of the opinions we discuss and the political decisions we take.

The only defence against the irrational movement of capital is voluntaristic political interventionism. Our primary objectives must be technological development, a rise in consumption, the fight against *la fracture sociale* or the social divide, and sustainable growth. Our first task is to identify those forces that can act positively, and not to confuse an active critique of finance capitalism and governmental irresponsibility with a general denunciation of the modern economy. Denunciations of that kind are as wrong as what they are attacking, and they recommend a return to the solutions of the past. Identifying the positive forces should free us from the irrationalism of populisms of all kinds.

Whether or not these populisms are trying to delude public opinion, and in particular the poorest categories, or whether they are the self-deluding discourses of those who have taken on the sacred mission of being prophets of doom in a world where nothing can be done to prevent the evil from spreading everywhere, is largely irrelevant. In any case, we must break with these illusions, errors and denunciations. Adopting the opposite approach, we must once more prioritize the analysis of the facts and above all intellectual debate and the development of proposals for action. We do have a lot of room for manoeuvre. One might almost say that we have more and more room for manoeuvre, as growth now depends upon increasingly indirect factors. The expression 'sustainable growth' says it all. Modernization is no longer simply a matter of accumulating capital and labour, or of having roads, schools, a public administration and computers; we also need to ensure the survival of fragile systems with open borders that exist in a changing and unpredictable environment. We certainly do have to get out of the ruins and illusions of the voluntaristic mode of development of the postwar period. But it is more important still to rediscover the meaning of the possible, and to listen to the social and moral demands without which it is quite impossible to resist the formidable pressures of a capitalist system which now extends to the whole planet.

In this context, the question that gives this book its title takes on its full meaning: how can we get beyond neoliberalism?

Unfortunately, some countries, and especially France, have to resolve two very different problems at the same time. They must get away from neoliberalism at a time when they have scarcely set foot in it. (There is something ridiculous about talk of extreme neoliberalism in a country where the state still controls half its resources, either through the welfare system or by intervening in economic life.) Those countries that have yet to abandon the old system of social controls over the economy and are reluctant to create a new system are in the most difficult situation of all. They are in danger of surrendering to an unfettered capitalism at the very moment when they are seeing the emergence of a radical opposition which rejects both modernization and capitalism, and confuses the necessary revenge of the excluded with the perpetuation of corporatisms and vested interests. The most important and dangerous form of populism is that expressed by the National Front, but other forms of populism are developing on the far left too. At a time when French society is, in practice, behaving more creatively than its pseudo-theorists and is capable of reconciling economic efficiency with new demands that could open the way to new social policies, populisms of every kind obscure our difficulties and therefore make them insoluble.

We are living in an unstable equilibrium because we are to some extent still living, both in real life and inside our heads, under the state that oversaw postwar reconstruction. At the same time, we are already living in a new international environment and a different cultural space. This process cannot be reversed. Our economic practices and the state of public opinion have certainly been sufficiently transformed to inject a satisfactory dynamism into French society. The long-term absence of any political action capable of reconciling economic goals with social objectives has, however, encouraged all kinds of attachment to the past and all kinds of populism. It is as though our only choice were one between a stateless capitalism and a Jacobinism that openly contradicts our practices and our lived experience.

If a surrender to unfettered capitalism were our only future, I would choose to make an alliance with the old republicans or the populists of the left. But only the most extreme intellectual dishonesty can convince us that we are faced with such an alternative. At the end of the nineteenth century, when capitalism was developing so vigorously, we saw the introduction of social legislation and then, on a larger scale, the creation of an industrial democracy. The social democracies of the early twentieth century were its heirs. At no point during this whole period was intellectual life reduced to an obstinate rejection of industrial civilization. Why should things be any different today? The immediate response is: because national political powers have become impotent, and because European institutions are effective only when they promote the free circulation of capital and the integration of an

economic space that is as big as North America. I say again
that this vision is devoid of any foundations. There is still a
political space between the international economy and our
personal lives, and it is by no means an empty space even
though the transition from dealing with the problems of industrial society to dealing with those of the information society, or from dealing with the problems of the administered
economy to dealing with those of the market economy, is slow
and difficult.

We are told that we have to make some decisive choices:
economic competitiveness or social welfare, building Europe
or national identity. This plunges us into despair or confusion
because we do not want to abandon any of these objectives,
even though we are told they are incompatible. Let us free
ourselves from these terroristic discourses and artificial di-
chotomies.

No one believes that the product of our activity is used
only for international trade on the one hand and to finance
the social security system on the other. Do we have to defend
at all cost the bad management of public sector companies,
urban segregation, the archaic recruitment of elites, and administrative obstacles to innovation? Are technological innovation, the expansion of the home market, and the way we
pay our taxes and social security contributions so irrelevant to
the competitiveness of the French economy? It is not as though
it could be steered and managed solely from the outside, or
by the famous international markets. Does it have to be pointed
out yet again that at least two-thirds of our foreign trade takes
place within the European Union and that a much higher proportion takes place within a bloc made up of Western Europe
and the United States?

Polemics that blame French bureaucracy for everything or
the equally extreme discourse that attributes all our woes to
the opening up of international markets may satisfy those who
have come up against bureaucratic absurdities or who have
been made unemployed because their companies have re-
located. But such perfectly understandable reactions become
absurd when they claim to explain everything. They can even
become scandalous: what right do we have, for instance, to

condemn the networked companies whose policies have played a central role in the emergence of the new industrial countries, when our balance of trade with those countries usually shows a surplus? Are we really defending the social security system by keeping it in its current state and refusing to reform it, when it produces the mediocre results with which we are all too familiar, and when our hospitals are too small or have too few patients to attract adequate resources and skilled personnel?

Refusing to choose between Market and State does not mean that centrism is our only option.

We have to stop being so frightened that we do nothing. The dangers are many, but we are not short of choice either. So let us get rid of both *la pensée unique* and *la contre-pensée unique*. Let us make a distinction between good and bad ways out of the neoliberal transition, out of this painful but necessary transition between one way of putting social controls on the economy and another, between one political space and another.

2

Four exits

Let's not go over it all again. While we can congratulate ourselves on the fact that market forces have helped to do away with harmful economic and social protectionisms, that does not necessarily mean that we can therefore reduce society to a market and accept the removal of all political and social controls on the economy. It is futile to evoke the confused idea of globalization to mask the damage being done by an unbridled capitalism which is increasingly finance-based and which threatens the economic growth of many countries, their attempts at reconstruction and the reappearance of aspirations which have for a long time been drowned by the absence of hope.

This position is not my point of arrival; on the contrary, it is my point of departure, and we know that today's political and intellectual debate is not centred on the condemnation of neoliberalism. The eminently liberal Tony Blair by no means thinks that the market will solve society's problems, and nor does the Brazilian centrist Fernando Henrique Cardoso or the Chinese government. The triumph of capitalism has been so costly and intolerable that everyone, on all sides, is trying to find a way out of the 'neoliberal transition'. But some cures are worse than the disease, and others are ineffective. Let us try to find the right exit.

Backwards

One's first reaction to the increasingly rapid growth in world trade – which has so many positive features – is to defend an identity, a history or a language. When we react in this way, truth and falsehood, and the useful and the dangerous, are so closely intertwined that it is impossible either to agree or to disagree. No one has the right to ask the French to dissolve their national consciousness and organization into an imaginary world society. But this defence of the nation is positive only if, rather than extolling an identity, it results in the democratic and national management of both the economy and social change. Of course the current trend towards the dualization of our societies, which is making them more and more like Latin American societies, must be resisted; yes, the defence of a living national identity and of the action of the nation-state is an integral part of what we call development.

We must also construct a new system of economic controls that has nothing in common with the system that has been collapsing for the last twenty years, and we must transcend the rhetorical opposition between Market and State. We must begin by refusing to preserve intact the decayed remains of the administered economy. Defending the most underprivileged does not mean backing strike calls from Air France pilots, particularly when we all know that they will have to go back to toeing the line. For their part, the civil service unions, which are now the biggest in France, both use revolutionary language to defend their legitimate interests, and protect the vested interests that are widening the social divide between those who enjoy job security and the rest.

What I am attacking here is not resistance to change or the discrepancy between fiery words and purely defensive actions; it is the way we call upon the state to subordinate economic, social and cultural problems to its own statist logic, which is at once national and bureaucratic. This is an old remedy, and it does a lot to explain why France is so behind the times in terms of economic, social and cultural modernization.

Even at the end of the nineteenth century, France was so

preoccupied with reinforcing the republican state and resisting the power of the church that it took little interest in the social question, or in other words the exploitation of workers. Its action was, as it happens, quite justified, as it put an end to clericalism and the scandalous condemnation of Dreyfus, but it led France to forget the need to organize a powerful labour movement. The left was anticlerical and colonialist, but it often forgot to be social. As a result, France fell far behind Great Britain and Germany in terms of unionization and social legislation. It was only in 1936 and 1945 that France voted through a body of social laws, and it did so on the initiative of the state rather than under pressure from social actors. The world wars strengthened this trend and the Gaullist and Communist joint management of post-Liberation France took to extremes the opposition between the state, which was viewed as an agency of the universal and of citizenship, and civil society, which was reduced to meaning the defence of particular interests. This discourse is heard whenever the public sector reasserts that it is the site of freedom and that its primary function is to protect citizens against profit and inequality. For a long time, and perhaps until the Vilvorde episode,[1] Renault and Peugeot seemed to be different types of companies, and the distribution of a public utility like gas enjoyed greater prestige than the production of bread.

What has to be challenged is the idea, which is so widespread in France, that the categories of the political are more important than those of social life. The republican idea asserts, for instance, that the social world must be subordinated to the political world, just as sociology must be subordinate to philosophy. Now this idea has gradually begun to have negative effects. While it is true that no society can be free or democratic unless it can invoke a higher principle of equality, proclaimed in advance, such as equality in the eyes of the law, it is also true that there is always a danger that such principles will become disconnected from social realities.

France is the country that proclaimed political rights most loudly, but it has never been very good at applying them in concrete social situations. What, said those who worked in the National Workshops, is the point of being citizens if we have to work in exhausting conditions or be denied work? This led to capitalist industrialization's first great social crisis: the days of June 1848. They were followed by the Paris Commune and its repression, which was applauded by many republicans. Karl Marx, who was the best observer of events in France between 1848 and 1871, rightly criticized the French 'political illusion' which led, for example, the young Paris Commune to expel the representatives of the Internationale from its ranks.

This way of thinking takes different forms and is present in almost every sector of public opinion. The underlying argument is that responsibilities, conflicts and solutions all lie within the sphere of the state. Nothing could be more common than criticisms of technocrats combined with calls for the state to fight market forces. We have often heard the state bourgeoisie being condemned in the name of the state petty bourgeoisie, to borrow a phrase from Pierre Bourdieu. Particularly in 1995. It is as though the state petty-bourgeoisie were not itself part of the state, and as though it were not trying to impose its own categories on social reality, as we see happening in education and in state agencies that deal with the economic sphere.

If we trap ourselves into making exclusive reference to the state, we expose ourselves to certain contradictions. Is the state anticapitalist, or is it technocratic and therefore statist? In a period of unemployment and job insecurity, will greater state intervention always be an effective way of helping the weakest, or will it make the members of the state apparatus stronger at every level? And if it is not, as I believe, contradictory to try to defend the social security system and at the same time to strengthen the productive sector, the pursuit of both these objectives must surely mean that we must be critical of the many state interventions that do nothing to improve either economic efficiency or social justice.

Those who refer only to the state, and who both attack and defend it, are the last representatives of the postwar mode of government. At a time when almost all countries were either in ruins or had been only recently established, the role of the state was, of necessity, central. The state's most extreme critics and its most arrogant defenders have a lot in common and they share the same inability to understand that the role of the state, which was once the central agency for modernization and reforms, was long ago replaced (successfully so in most countries) by the conflictual and dynamic combination of a competitive economy and social movements that are both trying to free themselves from state patronage and to resist those who conform to a truly capitalist logic. The constant appeal to the state considerably weakens economic actors, and it is an even greater obstacle to the formation of new social actors. One can understand why railway workers defend the rights they have won, but it is dangerous to see them as representatives of the excluded.

The social conflicts of the postwar period were mainly about the distribution of the products of growth. Today's social conflicts obey two very different logics: resisting the dualization of society on the one hand and, on the other, asserting cultural rights in a country which is not only increasingly multicultural but also one in which the assertion of personal rights is becoming more important than attempts to ensure that resources are distributed fairly.

The republican spirit has long resisted the demand for cultural rights and refused to defend minorities and differences. It has, in other words, refused to recognize human rights within the cultural domain. On the contrary, it sang the praises of a one and indivisible France, usually in order to destroy particular loyalties. It is only now that we are beginning to realize that this rigidity must be relaxed and that our practices must be more open and sensitive to diversity. Similarly, the Republican school claimed to be the people's school, even though state schools for a long time perpetuated the existence of two distinct sectors: the primary-vocational sector and the secondary-higher, as Baudelot and Establet put it. Eminently republican ministers have, finally, taken repressive measures against foreigners. This republican reaction is in fact neither right-wing nor left-wing; it is simply backward looking.

The idea of equality has strength only if it actively opposes inequalities. This is the very definition of fairness. For decades, the republican left applauded state schools' success in promoting equality. French sociologists from Naville to Girod, from Bourdieu to Boudon and from Baudelot and Establet to Prost and Dubet have demonstrated, first, that they did more to transmit inequality than to lessen it and, more recently, that they actually increased inequality and that it would be a mistake to relieve them of all responsiblity, as though they were just perpetuating inequalities of birth. These observations lead us to accept the need for a policy of 'reparation', or what we call 'positive discrimination' and what the Americans call 'affirmative action', though it would be simpler to call it 'fairness'. *La pensée unique's* denigrators claim that the word is a betrayal of the Republic. Do we therefore have to cast opprobrium on the work of John Rawls because we find at its heart the notion of fairness, which is, as it happens, closely bound up with the social-democratic tradition. Was it an aberration to introduce a lower than average retirement age for miners when, as was the case with other categories of workers who carried out physically and mentally demanding jobs, their life expectancy was shorter than that of other wage-earners? The compensatory measures that were taken were inspired by the idea of fairness, whereas the broader appeal to equality does nothing to reduce real inequalities. It is all very well to say that foreigners who come to France because they feel their lives are in danger must be welcomed and that they, or at least any of their children who are born in France, must be granted French nationality rapidly or even automatically, but the noble discourse that proclaims France to be the land of freedom by identifying it with universal values has led to their forced assimilation, or in other words has forced them to renounce all particular identities, rather as though integration and the defence of identity obeyed two contradictory logics. To put it more brutally, France is rejecting more and more of the foreigners living here on the grounds that the majority of French people think that if you do not have both feet on French soil you should be kicked out. We in fact know full well that, unlike a door, a society must be both open and closed.

Fortunately, real life in France goes on regardless of these declarations of principle, but they have left France ill-prepared for the most important demand of the moment: the right to be both equal and different. Women were the first to demand and obtain, though not without difficulty, that right. In a situation where we have to reconcile diversity and unity, and in which it is no longer possible to confine diversity to private life because it has invaded public life, appeals to the one and indivisible Republic sound like an antimodern rhetoric characterized by an obsession with the past.

France is the only country in Europe to feel that it has been living through a crisis for the last twenty years. And not without reason, as France is doing all it can to defend itself against new ideas, new economic strategies and relevant answers to the new needs of education. This is not to say by any means that we must give in to neoliberalism, but it is absurd to defend 'the French exception' in all circumstances.

The republican spirit also manifests itself in other and less extreme forms, but they too help to exacerbate the social crisis. The republican spirit insists on keeping out of the most acute conflicts, and it distances itself both from unfettered neoliberalism, which is in fact more verbal than real, and the very radical and critical actions that have been initiated with regard to the world of politics. It thus identifies with a centrism whose sole preoccupation is to re-establish order and security and to ensure that both the strong and the weak respect the law. This obviously results in more concrete and repressive measures being taken against the latter than the former. The republican spirit thus revives the long tradition of indifference to, or suspicion of, struggles for social and cultural rights, and that tradition has always forced demand-based movements to employ the language of revolution or even to become dependent upon parties – large or small – that are themselves revolutionary.

One has a definite feeling that public opinion is tired of debates for and against *la pensée unique*. The corollary of this boredom may be the very positive desire for concrete, if limited, measures that have visible effects, but it may also lead to a refusal to come to terms with the most serious social problems and to give a new priority to the defence of civic-mindedness and the fight against crime.

For many who prioritize the restoration of public order,

authority and security, these objectives do not have repressive or reactionary connotations. But how can we fail to see that they represent a return to the old theme of the dangerous classes, which were a perceived threat to the middle classes or the bourgeoisie, as we used to call them? And given that, in the nineteenth century, the formation of the labour movement reduced the size of the dangerous classes and that the action of the proletariat reduced the violence of the subproletariat, should we not be adopting the same line of conduct today? At a time when no new social movements are emerging or being recognized and when no serious reforms are being implemented, tirades about the crisis of authority, facile hedonism, the rejection of collective discipline and the cult of diversity still smack strongly of a taste for moral order, whether their authors want them to or not. And that may lead us to repress or fail to recognize the positive demands that are being put forward amid more panicky responses to the crisis in those milieus that are most affected by poverty, discrimination and social unrest.

The many intellectuals, elected politicians and trade unionists who are calling for a return to the basic values of the Republic would be more convincing if they admitted, when they discuss education, that there is a serious crisis in our schools. They are obviously not unaware of the fact that schools are doing even less now than in the past to reduce social inequality, and that in an uncertain world, having family support is more decisive for a child than a willing submission to the demands of reason. And yet . . .

When, in his 1998 report on our *lycées* and in his replies to his critics, Philippe Meirieu reminds us that, if we wish to evaluate schools, it is impossible to talk about acquisition of knowledge and the role of teachers unless we also take into account the social and individual conditions in which children live, he is saying something so obviously true that it is difficult to see who could challenge his analysis. He denounces certain practices for being too liberal, and who would refuse to agree with him in condemning both forms of non-communication: spontaneism and trapping teachers into a clerical role that obliges them to teach but not to educate?

Discussions of education and proposed reforms evoke such exasperation or even indignation that it is sometimes forgotten that the universal value of knowledge is not self-evident, and that knowledge had a directly emancipatory effect only at the time when society was fragmented and dominated by hereditary powers and hierarchies. In our society, pleasure on the one hand and the desire for a successful career on the other play such an important role that references to knowledge will come to mean less and less if we fail to take into consideration the motives as well as the constraints that are associated with any learning process and, in short, any effort. The mission of the 'black hussars'[2] was to destroy local and clerical mechanisms of social control and to associate faith in science with the building of a republican nation. They have accomplished that mission. But while they are still noble, these objectives cannot be achieved if we do not put pedagogical communication, and therefore children, at the centre of educational practice.

I once took part in a meeting of teachers, *lycée* students, representatives of their parents, unionists and politicians organized in the Orléans-Tours regional education authority to discuss the findings of the nationwide consultation carried out by Philippe Meirieu and the members of his commission. No one denied the fact that two themes dominated the pupils' answers: they wanted greater personal autonomy and better communication with their teachers. How can anyone claim that these demands pose an obstacle to access to knowledge and to the disciplines it requires?

Those who are scandalized by the idea of child-centred education are expressing a real fear. They are afraid that the old school system, or the image we have of it, will be swamped or even destroyed by the cultural transformations and social crises we are going through. They prefer to cling to the ideal image of this badly dented model because they are afraid of being swept away by the chaos that may well result from the development of spontaneism on the one hand and communitarianism on the other.

Why the pessimism? We must neither indulge in gloom-mongering nor believe that we are powerless against market forces or the forces of the bureaucratic state. On the contrary, we must assert that, in education and elsewhere, the vital thing is to regard individuals and groups as potential actors and not simply as victims who are either in chains or being manipulated. On the basis of that shared conviction, it will be possible to implement reforms that really will reduce inequality, eliminate exclusion, and increase everyone's capacity to take the initiative. There is no reason to see the three objectives as contradictory.

Downwards

Given that globalization is the ideology of the dominant forces and of all those who dream of ever more efficient systems of communication that will destroy in their wake all subjectivity, all social welfare, all collective memories and all personal projects, our salvation must come from the dominated and those who support them.

The idea that the slave alone, and not the master, is in a position to understand their relationship and therefore to transform it is as true today as it was in Hegel's day. New social movements capable of triggering political reforms must indeed take shape. The dominated must, however, have something to defend. At the same time, they must speak in the name of society as a whole. They must be, and must see themselves as, the defenders of equality, the right to work, the right to be different and the right to live in security. Those who can be defined by what they have lost have never been the actors of their own liberation. Their revolt could at best reveal the contradictions of the dominant system, but it was the new political and intellectual elites who used their rebellion and their poverty to establish a new power which they defined as more rational, more national or more in keeping with the will of God. The powers that emerged when power was seized by violence and in the name of a dominated, exploited and alienated people became totalitarian. The state they had conquered silenced the society and the people in whose name they spoke, and it soon declared war both at home and abroad on those they called the enemies of the people because they rejected their absolute power over the people.

Whenever the suffering of the dominated, the exploited or the excluded bursts on to the stage of history, history hesitates between the formation of a social movement and the irruption of ideologies and political forces that reduce the dominated to misery. What is the difference between the two processes? In the first, the dominated defend positive interests which the whole of society regards as such and recognizes as legitimate. It was not proletarians, building labourers or women in textile mills who built the labour movement and finally succeeded in establishing the idea of social rights. It was done by those who had a craft to defend and who refused to conform to the norms of production set by the logic of profit. And it was not, as Frantz Fanon believed, those people in the colonies who were furthest removed from colonial domination, or most strongly rooted in a different culture, who launched the national liberation movements. They were launched by people who had received a formal education, usually in the colonial country, and who were aware of their rights.

There is now a great danger that the dominated will not be able to create new social movements because they are defined by their exclusion, or by the fact that they have been denied work or the papers that would allow them to lead a normal life in our country. This is why our main problem is, and will long remain, this: how do we move from exclusion to protest, from isolation to the call for rights that are recognized by all, and from periodic revolts to sustained political action?

This shift and the emergence of new social movements are taking place before our very eyes, and chapter 3 of this book will be devoted to them. But before we can initiate emancipatory actions, we have to overcome a certain number of obstacles. Above all, we must avoid what we have already identified as the backward-looking solutions advocated by those who want at all cost to defend the interests and values of the state petty bourgeoisie in a world where the globalization of the economy, the increase in exclusion and poverty and the rise of nationalisms threaten what they call the Republic.

It is now high time to describe the second danger that threatens the emerging movements, and therefore democracy itself: populism. Although it can be found in very different countries and very difficult historical moments, populism has always meant the rejection of all institutions and all systems of representation in the name of the essence of the people. It also means the rejection of any attempt at free thought. Populism is an incantatory appeal to popular forces, but its goal is to reduce them to silence by establishing a system of absolute domination. The people need a leader, individual or collective, to rid them of those who are using them for their own advantage. The people need a leader who can allow them to recover their identity and become aware of their strength. Such is the populist credo.

Populism is neither of the right nor of the left, since it exists outside the categories of political representation. While populism is conspicuously visible on the fringes of the right, it can also be found on the fringes of the left. It is to the left of the left, and to the right of the right. In contemporary France, the National Front represents the most highly organized form of populism. It is made up of fascist groups, traditionalist Christians and Poujadists, but it also feeds on, on the one hand, the despair and worries of industrial society's population at large and, on the other, the crisis within a parliamentary right which has disintegrated because it clung to its Gaullist heritage of social nationalism at the very time when it was trying to implement a neoliberal economic policy. The National Front represents an expression of negativity, rejection and exclusion rather than a programme for managing the transformations that are turning all societies upside down.

Other forms of populism have appeared in the ranks of the ultra-left, which is against both the plural left and globalization. These forms of populism do more to denounce rulers than to encourage autonomous action on the part of the ruled. They distrust representative institutions and believe in the need for violence. They are quite prepared to attack those intellectuals who are convinced of the importance of the new movements, just as the communists used to spend their time attacking the socialists they denounced as 'social-traitors', when they should have been forming an alliance with them to block the rise of fascism in the 1920s and 1930s.

The capacity of the dominated to take action is weak when they define themselves solely in terms of the identity they have been denied. This leads to a proliferation of minipopulisms which are not to be confused with actions whose primary task is to enhance the capacity of dominated or excluded categories to intervene. Such policies of denunciation and rejection have often taken precedence over the formation of new actors. To take an example to which we will return. While Aides has succeeded in enabling homosexuals to become actors who are playing a full part in the transformation of attitudes and behaviour, and in the management of their illness in cases where they are suffering from AIDS,[3] Act Up won a higher profile by confining itself to denunciation. We must therefore be wary of jumping to conclusions. To say that Aides is moderate and that Act Up is radical is meaningless, as the two organizations are moving in different directions. Act Up is moving towards a stance of total rejection, while Aides is moving towards the awakening of the public's conscience and the transformation of laws and moral attitudes. Even if Act Up's voice has been more widely heard, the work of Aides has achieved much more, since public opinion, at the very time when AIDS was spreading, stopped blaming the 'queers' and recognized their right to live their lives as they saw fit.

Having mentioned this relatively limited but exemplary instance, how can we fail to think of May '68? The way we commemorate its emancipatory achievements has given rise to a disturbing concensus. It has taken thirty years for the anti-authoritarian movement symbolized by Daniel Cohn-Bendit to be recognized as May '68's most important actor. At the time, and for the long decade that followed, the workerist revolutionism of the Trotskyists and Maoists seemed to be the principal aspect of the student-worker movement.

The explanation for this historical misunderstanding is the higher profile of revolutionary ideologies in a country which, as I have often said, is more interested in the state than in society, in political action than in trade unionism and in calls for unity than in the recognition of diversity.

The *groupuscules* are now back and some veterans of 1968 are resurfacing. It should, however, be noted that the best known of them, namely Alain Krivine, has demonstrated both foresight and prudence. The eternal components of populism – direct action, the rejection of all forms of representation, strategies designed to grab the attention of the media and the critique of intellectuals – are all present today and may obscure something that is much more important in both material and political terms: the formation of social movements based upon the universalist defence of rights that must be granted to all.

The movement of 'those without papers' (*les sans papiers*) merits our full attention because it was able to convince the majority of us that through their action the excluded, who are by definition in the minority, were defending the basic rights of all. They were able to mobilize that conviction to win support for people who faced being arrested by the police, even though they had taken refuge in a church. And the reason why the mobilization was at its height when the repeal of Article 1 of the Debré law was put on the agenda is that those French people who did have papers felt that they too were threatened by attacks on people who, because they had no papers, had no rights and therefore could not have access to either work or welfare.[4]

To digress for a moment. It seems to me essential to speak of exclusion and of the fight against exclusion, despite the relevance of Robert Castel's criticisms of the use that is sometimes made of the word. I use it because it refers to the act of 'excluding', whereas 'marginality' does no more than designate a situation. To speak of exclusion is to name, or at least to seek, an adversary and therefore to begin to act against exclusion. And that is how the word is used: just like the word 'justice', it connotes protest and anger. To demand justice is to accuse those who have wronged a victim. A victim who

uses the word 'justice' becomes an actor. Opposing exclusion
also means demanding citizenship and the right to take part
in political, economic or cultural life. The word is therefore
such a natural part of the thesis I am defending that it seems
to me essential to use it.

The strength of these grassroots movements, which have
been supported by democratic initiatives including the petitions drawn up by film-makers, artists and intellectuals, may
have temporarily concealed the profound difference between
the populist ideology of radical rejectionism and the defence
of universal rights. We are now seeing the appearance of texts
in which we can hear discourses imbued with a hardline
populism. They are full of denunciations and devoid of analysis. It is of course much easier to attack intellectuals and
journalists than to analyse an economic situation. A short time
ago, Viviane Forrester's book *The Economic Horror*[5] found a
vast audience because it attacked the workings of the global
economy and denounced intolerable situations, but it had no
analysis and no solution to offer.

As in the early 1970s, the political left's ability to react may
do something to limit the damage that is being done by this
populism. Just as the Common Programme of the Left helped
France to avoid terrorism – an extreme form of populism that
affected Germany and especially Italy – so the formation of
the plural left[6] has until now prevented the emerging social
movements from being structured into a truly populist ultra-
left political movement.

The populist threat is greater in the movements of the homeless and the unemployed than in that of the *sans papiers*, which
was based on the mobilization of a moral conscience. Can we
solve the housing crisis by occupying empty blocks of flats?
Obviously not, and no one has in fact said that we can. But
some people have been seduced by the idea that spectacular
denunciations are enough to solve problems. Mobilizing against
unemployment is more difficult still, as unemployment is a
product of both the changes that have occurred in the world
economy, and the inadequacy of French policy with regard to
management, education and the distribution of resources. That
is why, in the wake of the initiatives taken by Maurice Pagat,

the occupation of the offices of ASSEDIC (Association pour l'Emploi dans l'Industrie et la Commerce: the state agency responsible for unemployment insurance payments) had such a major impact. Other spectacular actions of the day, such as the occupation of the École Normale Supérieure, had a high populist content, but were not guided by any practical considerations.

The populist deviation is, on the other hand, absent from the Seine-Saint-Denis teachers' movement, which has had strong support from pupils' parents, and from lycée students. Born of a demand for equality and the claim that the state spends less per child in poor *départements* than in rich ones (which is true), this movement has the support of elected communist politicians as distinguished as M. Braouezec, the mayor of St Denis. It has reached the conclusion that there is a need for positive discrimination, or to give more to those who have less. This quest for fairness is the antithesis of populism. In the autumn of 1998, the *lycéens* also protested against disruption in schools because its effects are felt mainly by the most underprivileged.

Are we to come to the optimistic conclusion that populism (of both the ultra-right and the ultra-left) is weaker than it is usually believed to be, and that its different variants will not prevent the emergence of social movements and the renewal of political life? I think that we can.

The main threat obviously comes from the ultra-right, but there are reasons for hoping that the National Front will break up, because many of its activists are beginning to find its political impotence intolerable. As for the ultra-left, it is more difficult to make a prognosis, as the categories involved are weak and scattered. Populism is a reaction to the extreme disruption of political action over the last twenty-five years, and it will become less of a temptation only if the political left in France and elsewhere can demonstrate that the internationalization and deregulation of the economy do not condemn us to political impotence and that globalization will lead to an increase in exclusion only if we are incapable of demonstrating any political will.

At a time when the single currency is coming into being

thanks to a gigantic operation that is seriously disrupting the state's traditional modes of action, the idea that we are politically impotent naturally occurs to both those who believe that we can return to the voluntarism of de Gaulle and the Communists, and those who think that the only solution is to reject the changes that are going on, to denounce those who are introducing them and to despise intellectuals who will not resign themselves to despair and self-flagellation. In its own way, the populist tumult signals a change of era marked by the liquidation of forms of state intervention that have become ineffective or negative, and by the formation of new social actors and new political strategies that can launch new actions to promote social integration, economic modernization and respect for cultural rights.

Upwards

The new technological leap forward our societies are taking has to be given a positive welcome. And while it is legitimate to evaluate the risks inherent in the possible misuse of science, and especially biology, there are no grounds for losing our faith in scientific research. We have strong criticisms to make of television, but it would not, I think, enter anyone's mind to give clerics – religious or secular – a monopoly on information. We know that our schools increase inequality rather than reducing it, but who would dare to oppose the general raising of educational standards?

Only a few years ago, this acceptance of the future and this rejection of the models we have inherited from the past would not have been taken for granted, and it was therefore necessary to defend the need for them. The priority must now be to criticize the complacent enthusiasm for modernity which fails to come to terms with the forms of power and conflict it will bring. And while we do have to break with the past, we also have to reject the idea that technological innovations and the acceleration of international economic commerce will automatically give birth to a new democracy, this time on a world scale because the national level, as they never tire of telling us, no longer corresponds to the nature of economic networks and exchanges (which are by their very nature transnational).

Jacques Delors has to be given the credit for the idea of constructing a European social model. Unfortunately, his White Book was, as we know, put back on the shelf after his departure from office and, since then, debates about Europe have concentrated almost exclusively on the single currency and finance. It is true that the French government has stressed the need for a real economic government for Europe and that it rightly opposed the proposal that the governor of the central European bank should be designated by the governors of the national central banks. But how can we fail to see that building Europe is devoted essentially to ensuring freedom of movement for capital, that the coordination of trade unions at the European level has had no great effect, and that the European Parliament is far from playing the same role at the European level that national parliaments play in their respective countries. Like republicanism and populism, worldism is one of the infantile disorders of the new society we have entered. And globalism certainly poses as great a threat to the revival of democracy as republicanism and populism, because it obviously serves the interests of the dominant economic (and especially financial) forces.

No miracle can ensure that democratic life will be the life-blood of tomorrow's very hypothetical world society. On the contrary, democratic life will remain bound up with national institutions and it will be strengthened at the local level thanks to voluntary organizations, most of them founded for local reasons. If it does not surrender to the populist temptation, the revival of public life that we are already beginning to see will go hand in hand with the increasingly important role played by indirect development factors, especially if renewed growth allows governments to allocate more resources to improving the social welfare system and taking new initiatives to modernize our hospitals and schools.

To claim that the way out of our current difficulties is upwards is an illusion. We cannot expect technology or economic forces to solve social problems. They may even make them insoluble if public opinion becomes convinced that economic progress requires only freedom and flexibility to improve all our lives.

I will not dwell here on the modernizing illusion, as it has already lost much of its power. Indeed, its influence was always confined to very restricted circles as public opinion was too preoccupied with the crisis to be taken in by a sociological fantasy. As a result, we are only too ready to condemn modernization out of hand. We cannot, however, criticize those who condemn it unless we also denounce the idea that technological and economic transformations will automatically bring us affluence, freedom and happiness.

Towards the possible

The monetary unification of the greater part of Europe will not resolve the economic and social problems of the participating countries, but it will put an end to some outdated debates. It will shut the door on the past and force us to think about and organize the future. Rather than dreaming of a radiant future of one kind or another, we will have to reconstruct our political and social life.

Fortunately, the three dangers that threaten us – republicanism, populism and worldism – are so different that they cannot come together to offer the people of France a new policy. While republicanists and populists have united from time to time, as when they opposed the Maastricht treaty for example, everyone knows that there can be no lasting agreement between those who believe that economic neoliberalism can solve social problems, and those who want at all cost to subordinate the economy to a state they see as an enlightened despot or, which comes down to the same thing, a republican monarchy. If, however, we adopt the viewpoint of the emerging social movements, it becomes equally clear that the one thing that these three temptations do have in common is that they paralyse social actors and distract them from their goals.

France has narrowly avoided disaster. It was not the state of the French economy or the crisis in the social security system that brought it to the edge of the abyss. It was the fact that public opinion was trapped in an impasse. For twenty years, a great number of French citizens were indeed convinced that our social security policy and the world economic system had become incompatible. Some took this view because they saw globalization as a form of economic management that would inevitably reduce employment, social welfare and wage levels; others took the same view because they were convinced that only market forces could do away with corporatism, bureaucracy and budgetary deficits.

So long as the idea prevailed that the contradiction between economic necessities and social objectives was insurmountable, all France could do was hobble towards disaster. Between 1991 and 1995, and then again in 1997, stagnation and unemployment, together with the weakness of government policies, all sapped our capacity for action. From the major crisis of 1995 until the sudden defeat of the right in 1997, the country therefore appeared to be ungovernable, and France became more pessimistic as the creation of a single European currency began to look inevitable.

That period is now over. This is not because effective measures have finally been taken, and nor is it simply because the international economic conjuncture has improved (France has yet to be seriously affected by the crises in Asia and Russia) and because domestic consumption and investment have risen. It is because a government has at last dared to say that social progress and economic realism are not incompatible, and that they can and must go hand in hand. This has allowed France to join the leading pack of those European countries that have for years been demonstrating with some success that it is possible to reconcile the two.

During their first year in government, Lionel Jospin, Martine Aubry and Dominique Strauss-Kahn convinced France of their resolve to get out of the impasse. At the end of this period, encouraged by his success and his popularity, the Prime Minister spoke in more doctrinal terms and openly expressed his intention of reconciling social ends and economic means. He spoke of becoming a full member of the world economic system, and at the same time of his refusal to destroy the social welfare system, despite the neoliberals' repeated calls for its destruction. One can and must criticize the government when it proves to be weak, but one cannot overlook the fact that it has recreated a space for the art of possible.

We will, however, be able to play an effective part in the creation of new social actors only if majority opinion recognizes that the future is open and that we are not destined to fail. By rescuing us at the last moment from the contradictions and convulsions that were paralysing us, the present government has already made its contribution to giving a new meaning to analyses that speak in terms of social actors and social conflicts. That was all the more necessary in that, while it did cut the Gordian knot that was strangling us, the very same government has displayed serious reservations about the emerging social movements and even a certain hostility towards them.

There must now be an end to that hostility and the demands for the defence of rights must be listened to. But the government's reluctance to listen should also remind us that these movements must act independently and must not become a 'base' for any political party.

3
New social movements?

A misunderstanding

Three years after the great strike of December 1995, it is impossible to reflect on social movements, old or new, without analysing that movement in detail. This is not simply because it was on such a large scale, but also because it was the starting point for an ideological construct that developed all the more rapidly in that it existed in a vacuum. That is all the more surprising and regrettable in that real social movements were emerging at the same time, and were the products of long-term developments. The misunderstanding that I am denouncing is therefore twofold. On the one hand, we have a failure to understand the nature of the 1995 strike movement; on the other, we have an inability to see that there was something new about the real social movements that were beginning to emerge.

Those who see the massive support given by public opinion to the December 1995 strike as a sign of renewed class struggle, or even union militancy, are indulging in wishful thinking. It is true that public opinion did support all the strikes of the day because it was worried and shocked by unemployment and job insecurity. It is also true that it gave particularly strong support to the December 1995 strike in order to express its discontent; but the fact remains that the real meaning of the strike itself is that it revealed the exhaustion and breakdown of what Guy Groux calls the social bloc, or in other words state management of social relations and labour relations in particular. This was a typically French model and it greatly weakened our trade unions, because it made the state the supreme guarantor of social progress. Social progress had to continue (and did continue), but neither the economic situation nor wage-earners' ability to negotiate was ever really taken into account. This model, which has always allowed political forces, and especially the state, to triumph over social or economic forces, has long been exhausted. It is in fact no longer the state that drives the economy. Even as early as 1981, it was an illusion to believe that large-scale nationalizations would help to modernize the economy. In the 1990s, by which point French companies were doing better in the international markets, it was clear both that the economic activity of the state consisted primarily in managing its own sector, and that it was increasingly bad at doing so.

There is a similar picture at the social level. The state, which once launched a dynamic employment policy and believed in the equalizing role of education, has long since been reduced to defending those sectors that are under its control, to making the nation as a whole bear most of the cost of public sector retirement pensions, and to allowing short-term limited contracts to invade both the public and private sector. The same state gives the educational system only a minor role in the training and retraining of wage-earners, and it recruits its elite in a conservative fashion.

France therefore found itself with almost no unions and an enfeebled state. From that point of view, the 1995 strike did not, as subsequent events demonstrated, mark the rebirth of unionism. It signalled the bankruptcy of a way of managing the economy and labour relations that had long been ineffective and even destructive. What is more important, it revealed the divisions that existed within a society which believed economic openness and social integration to be absolutely contradictory.

This interpretation does not for a moment question either the motives of the vast majority who supported the strike so strongly, or the state's desire to halt the deterioration of the social situation – and, therefore, of public morale. It is, on the other hand, an obvious challenge to the interpretation put forward at the time by those who claimed that the state should take more responsibility for managing both the economy and society. That could only hasten the destruction of economic and social actors.

I would also point out that, between 1995 and 1998, it became increasingly clear that the most significant conflicts had shifted from the field of social rights to that of cultural rights. These conflicting themes will be central to this chapter.

From classic struggles to new struggles

When we speak without further qualification of social movements, we suggest that social struggles have their unity, and that their unity is based upon a rejection of neoliberal policies which have the well-known effect of subordinating social life to the crushing logic of a globalization that forces down wages, increases unemployment, threatens the social security system and reduces the state's capacity to intervene. And indeed, how can we not defend social security and wage levels? How can we not be against unemployment and job insecurity? The problem is not only that such declarations of principle do not in themselves offer any solution; they also fail to recognize that, while they are by no means indifferent to these goals, many demonstrations of popular feeling are of a different nature. *They are demands for cultural rights.*

What might be called classical movements will be discussed here only to the extent that their action concentrates on the defence of working conditions and wages. In recent years, it is the truck-drivers' movement that has had the highest profile, and it was, despite the inconvenience it caused, supported by the population because the number of hours drivers were spending on the road seemed scandalous in a country which had an official working week of thirty-nine hours and which was about to reduce it to thirty-five hours. In short, the fact that this was a movement of the classical type by no means detracted from its importance.

Other movements, and there have been a lot of them, were launched in public sector companies and services, but they had nothing to do with the logic of neoliberalism. Both the RATP (the Paris transport system) and the EDF (the electricity board) are cases in point. In the case of the SNCF (national railway system), the issues at stake were railway workers' retirement arrangements and reforms to social security contributions. The movement representing junior doctors had even less to do with neoliberal economic policies, since it was not demanding better working conditions for hospital doctors (and conditions are indeed very bad), but higher salaries for doctors working in the private sector who were paid from the social security budget. It is pointless to dwell on the unrest at Air France. The movement of the unemployed, finally, is the only movement that is really in phase with the economic situation, and I will come back to it, but both its scale and its repercussions remained relatively limited.

The striking feature of developments since the early 1980s is that the movements that have had the greatest effect on public opinion because of their content, and not just their context, have usually been those formed to defend cultural rights. That is why I will begin by discussing the *beur* movement and the actions of antiracist activists, and then the homosexual movements associated with the fight against AIDS. Of all these *sans* ('without' or '-less') movements, it is obviously that of the *sans papiers* that has had – by far – the greatest impact. I will come back to this too.

What does this development mean? It obviously does not mean that the problems of jobs and wages are no longer important, but it does mean that the formation of actors, and therefore the renewal of public life, usually takes the form of a demand for cultural rights and that it is this kind of struggle, rather than movements that directly oppose the logic of neoliberalism, that deserve to be called 'social movements' because it goes without saying that social movements cannot exist unless they both assert something and reject something.

Can a collective action, to say nothing of a social movement, be based upon what people do not have, or on dependency or simply poverty? Some will say, 'of course' and then add: 'what else could it be based on?' Surely it was exploitation in the workplace that gave birth to the labour movement, colonial domination that gave rise to national liberation movements, and male domination that gave rise to the women's movement?

Although they are put forward as though they were so many truisms, these answers do not stand up to analysis. Opposition to domination is not enough to create a movement; a movement must put forward demands in the name of a positive attribute. Trade unionists defended labour and crafts against capitalist exploitation; anticolonial movements were inspired by an awareness of having a national or cultural identity; and it was the assertion of a specifically female personality that inspired women's struggles against their dependency. What is more, the struggle must not simply be a struggle against the ruling order; it must be waged in the name of values that are deemed central by the whole of society. The world of labour opposed the employers in the name of progress and industrial society; colonial domination was fought in the name of self-determination and therefore freedom. The women's movement affected the whole of society because it demanded the liberation of the body and of sexuality. Having defined the nature of social movements, we now have to look at how they are shaped, at the nature of their 'infantile disorders' and at the obstacles that prevent them from maturing.

The two major dangers that threaten the formation of new social movements are the lapse into violence and extreme dependency on outside supports. It is not easy to protect an embryonic movement from the outside groups that try to use it, or from the outbursts of violence that destroy it from within. These weaknesses and disorders are to be found in the *sans* movements: *sans logis, sans-papiers, sans-travail* (the homeless, the 'paperless' and the jobless). The important thing is, however, to recognize that although their actions appear to be based purely upon what these people do not have, they do contain positive demands, and are therefore expressions of major conflicts that make them central to society and culture.

This does not mean that we do not have to be on the look-out for deviations and especially the political or ideological manipulations to which movements that have as yet little autonomy can fall victim.

The most conspicuous and pronounced feature of contemporary struggles is the desire to rebel, reject and denounce. They are rebellions against the unbearable and the intolerable. But once they reject an order that excludes, they have to choose between two possible paths. One leads to the formation of autonomous social actors, reconciling their particular demands of what are usually minority groups with the defence of principles acknowledged by society, and more specifically of rights; the other leads to a dependency on ideological or political forces that do not believe in the possible formation of autonomous actors, and set themselves up as vanguards whose task it is to give a meaning, and sometimes even an organization, to mere 'forces' or 'masses' who cannot develop any self-consciousness. There are three component elements to the collective actions of recent years: a primal revolt, a recourse to a general principle of legitimacy and, at the opposite extreme, the instrumentalization of the collective action by powerful or educated vanguards.

The first and third of these component elements are easily understood. The first is the most obvious: any action is accompanied by acts of transgression and a refusal to obey the rules. Empty buildings and administrative offices are occupied, and demonstrations take place in the streets. The explanation for the third – dependency – is the weakness of these actions; as in the past, ideological, intellectual or religious groups still claim the right to define their meaning. It is, however, more difficult, and therefore more important, to explain what it is about these actions that allows the analyst to speak of a social movement. There is something very new about them.

The movements of industrial society, and above all the labour movement, spoke in the name of history, progress, the affluent society or communist society, or in other words in the name of a future that was desirable and even necessary. But the twentieth century was dominated to such an extent by totalitarian regimes predicting the coming of the perfect society and the new man that we can no longer go on believing in utopias that have catastrophic effects. On the contrary, we are acutely aware that our societies are fragile, and that they are threatened both by their internal disorder and the destruction of their environment. We are against the proliferation of technologies and unfettered liberalism, but we are also against those forms of communitarianism obsessively trading on identity that are gaining ground because they claim to be resisting the dictatorship of the markets. *The positive goal of today's social movements, which oppose both the reign of markets and the domination of communitarian-inspired movements, is the defence of the cultural and social rights of individuals and minorities.* These movements no longer speak in the name of the perfect society and they no longer look to the future; they are fighting for the universal right to lead a free and 'human' existence. The general principle on which all social movements are now based is the right to cultural equality.

Let us now look at a number of the collective actions of recent years and try to see beyond the primal revolt in order to distinguish between, on the one hand, the ideological domination that distorts and smothers them and, on the other hand, the new assertion of the rights of individuals and groups who have been crushed by the ruling order, inequality and exclusion. It is too easy to see only the weakness of such actions; what we have to understand is the social and political innovations they are making, even though they are limited, short-lived and usually dominated by outside groups.

The *beurs*

When immigrants, most of them from the Maghreb,[1] ceased to be regarded as immigrant workers and when France began to restrict immigration and to close its frontiers in 1974, they (and especially the second generation, or the children who were born in France) experienced a fairly rapid integration but they also found that a major section of the population rejected them. That reaction was not confined to the National Front itself. In the circumstances, it was not very difficult to foresee the emergence of a social movement which would combine an assertion of a cultural, ethnic and religious identity with a fight against xenophobia and racism, in the name of (cultural) human rights.

Such a movement did indeed take shape, but it quite rapidly disintegrated and gave way to more sporadic mobilizations against the National Front. They were at once more political and more media oriented. Let us recall the main events. Following a number of incidents, most of them violent, in the Les Minguettes area of Vénissieux (a suburb of Lyon), young Franco-Algerians, most of them living in difficult areas, founded a *beur* movement. After the attack on Toumi Djadja, who was the leader of SOS-Avenir Minguettes, it was decided to organize a march against racism and inequality. Strongly supported by the priest Christian Delorme, the idea overcame the scepticism with which it had initially been greeted, and the organizers succeeded in mobilizing 100,000 people for a demonstration in Paris. The march had the support of many important figures, most of them political, and delegates were received by President Mitterrand (who agreed to their request for the introduction of a ten-year resident's permit). The march became the kernel for SOS-Racisme, whose main founders were Julien Dray and Harlem Désir. SOS-Racisme spoke both of fraternity ('Hands off my pal') and of the recognition of the *beur* movement (the little yellow hand used as a logo by the movement was a 'hand of Fatima'). Its collective deliberations initially focused on the recognition of immigrant cultural identity by stressing the need for a new openness on the part of a republican spirit which was in general hostile to minorities.

The situation was, however, quickly reversed. Most of the left, and the whole of the right, felt threatened by the militant and aggressive Islamism that was developing all over the world and by the threat it represented to public freedoms. This reversal became obvious at the time of the 'headscarf affair'. Although most of the girls who wore *hijabs* to school were, as the interviews carried out by Françoise Gaspard and Farhad Khosrokhavar clearly demonstrated,[2] trying to integrate themselves into the world of the school without denying their own cultural identity, and although the Minister for Education, Lionel Jospin and the Conseil d'État adopted a position inspired by tolerance, a number of intellectuals, unionists and political figures strongly denounced a gesture that seemed to them to be incompatible with the republican spirit and secularism.

Attacked for the support it had given the *beurs*, SOS-Racisme retreated more and more, and reoriented itself towards the struggle *against* racism that replaced the movements *in favour* of the *beurs*. The action of the *beurs* themselves was rapidly forgotten and some of their leaders turned in disappointment to violence, while others turned to religion. From this point onwards, the struggle against the National Front, which had beeen growing steadily throughout this period and eventually won 15 per cent of the vote, imposed its own logic, and made the recognition of cultural identities impossible. Although immigrant associations demonstrated in Paris to defend the Kurdish and Kabyle causes, the struggle against the National Front was organized in the name of an increasingly restrictive republicanism, whilst the Front itself benefited from the fear and the rejection of foreigners inspired by rising unemployment and social unrest in the suburbs. This development was so rapid and so complex that the memory of the *beurs'* march of 1983 almost disappeared. More liberal minds consoled themselves by noting that French society seemed once more to be capable of absorbing a new wave of immigrants after half a century of turmoil. And yet, one could already see that young people of African or Arab origin were beginning to go back to Islam.

One can understand the political reasons why fear of Islamist terrorism and denunciations of the National Front were centre-stage. The fact remains that a potential social and cultural actor had been destroyed and that, for fear of multiculturalism, France had refused to recognize the cultural rights of immigrants and other minorities. This country was the first in Europe to proclaim the Rights of Man, but it was slow

to recognize the social rights of workers. It has been slower
still to recognize cultural rights, despite the positive actions
of enlightened defenders of secularism such as the Ligue
d'Énseignement.

Against AIDS

The balance sheet is more positive in the area of AIDS, as
actions have been linked to public recognition of homosexuals as social and political actors. This success is all the
more noteworthy in that, as Frédéric Martel has shown, representatives of homosexuals such as FHAR (Front Homosexuel
d'Action Révolutionnaire) and newspapers like *Gai pied* and
even gay businesses for a long time rejected specifically homosexual actions against AIDS because, being good republicans,
they were afraid of designating themselves as 'problem categories'.[3] It was only when it was recognized that there was a
need for a preventive policy that demanded the active involvement of the groups most concerned – homosexuals, drug
users and the recipients of multiple blood transfusions in particular – that a collective consciousness began to emerge. That
it did so was largely thanks to Aides, the organization founded
by Daniel Defert. Being oriented towards concrete goals, its
action was effective. Aides stressed the need for prevention,
but above all it provided help for people with AIDS and strug-
gled against the hostility and discrimination of sections of the
medical profession itself. Even so, self-imposed limitations
prevented Aides from becoming the voice of homosexual self-
assertion, and it has always had serious reservations about that
objective.
   Self-assertion was possible thanks to Act Up's more aggressive strategy, which was widely publicized by the media, and
also through some spectacular actions, and more carnivalesque
and commercial events. In both France and the United States,
Act Up's action is an example of vanguardism. Its provocations attract wide support but they do less than Aides's more
instrumental action to shape an awareness of being a collect-

ive actor. Homosexuals have also finally been recognized as gays, partly because the population felt compassionate towards the young men who were dying, but also because of the general relaxation of traditional moral norms. For a few years, or until it became a more commercial event, the Gay Pride march provided the main occasion for the expression of this openly demonstrated homosexual consciousness.

The final outcome has been positive. Homosexuals have acquired both rights – and are struggling to obtain more rights – and a collective cultural consciousness. But the various elements in the movement remain divorced from one another. Aides has worked mainly to shape a self-consciousness while Act Up has concentrated on combating adversaries. Actions that were less organized, but which did attract wide outside support, particularly from the Socialist Party, have resulted in some recognition of the cultural rights of homosexuals. This partial success can be judged satisfactory to the extent that gays and lesbians are asking for recognition rather than trying to transform society as a whole.

We have now reached the point where the creation of the PACS (Pacte Civile de Solidarité) – which grants homosexual couples certain rights, notably in the area of inheritance – is launching a debate that will question basic atttitudes (do homosexual couples have the right to bring up children?) in the same way that debates about contraception and abortion once did.[4] I mention these past debates because the one thing they have in common with the current debate is that most of the men and women who defended the right to abortion, for example, were convinced that everything should be done to prevent women from actually having to have abortions. In the case of homosexuals, the debate goes deeper: if we undermine the father/mother duality and completely divorce children from the complementary presence of a father and a mother, we are also undermining the very basis of our conception of what makes a person. And we are doing so not because we can do no other or by force of circumstance in the situations decribed above – and which are now commonplace – but as the result of a deliberate choice.

We have to start from a different principle, one that asserts the need for parity between men and women at the level of political institutions, or in other words at the level of the expression of the sovereignty of the people. According to this view, no manifestation of the human race is more general than the man/woman duality. It follows that, as beings who have a gender, men and women have equal rights but that there are de facto or natural differences between them. It is because they have equal rights but are at the same time different that men and women have the right to decide how to construct their sexual roles, and especially their parental roles, given that the complementary roles of fathers and mothers must still be regarded as a major precondition for the shaping of the personality. Minority categories may give rise to deviant situations, but they too can help to promote a stronger conception of parenthood that encourages parents to be more actively involved with their children.

The one thing that is certain is that the children of homosexual couples do encounter rejection. That is, however, an argument in favour of recognizing homosexual marriages: doing so would strike a blow against a form of discrimination that damages children. One cannot argue against this suggestion on the grounds that homosexuals living together under the terms of a PACS are in the same position as a great many heterosexuals, because the PACS could be criticized for being too close to the more familiar system of *concubinage* governing unmarried heterosexual couples. Homosexuals thus have to go on being a case apart, as it is the recognition that they have equal rights that is at issue; that is why homosexual marriages must be given the same recognition as heterosexual marriages.

The important thing about this debate, which has scarcely got under way in France, is that it demonstrates that questions of culture and personality are now at the centre of the political field. Something which is confirmed, to a certain extent, by the movements that defend the *sans*.

The *sans*

When the *sans-papiers*, some of them on hunger strike, are brutally evicted from the church where they have taken refuge, when spectacular occupations draw the attention of the media and the public to the high number of people who are homeless, and when the unemployed occupy the offices of the ANPE (Agence Nationale pour l'Emploi: the national employment agency) and ASSEDIC, it is clear that we are dealing with major struggles. Thanks to the media, they have been able to mobilize large sections of public opinion. But do these movements represent the emergence of new social actors, or are they signs of social crises?

The idea defended here is that a real social movement is indeed emerging, but that it is constantly threatened by ideological archaism or the radicalism of pure protest.

No event has a univocal meaning, and no event is a textbook example. One has only to recall the commentaries that were being made ten or twenty years after 1968, – and they were very different from those we hear today – to realize that it is absurd to think that events can speak for themselves. But the fact that historical or sociological analysis is never simply a matter of photographing events so as to bring out their *one* general meaning is no reason for abandoning the attempt to find their primary meaning or the emergent sense of new collective actions.

These movements are usually seen as having two main meanings. According to some commentators, globalization is now triumphant, just as finance capitalism was triumphant at the beginning of the last century. Given finance capitalism's unbridled power, radical protests and revolutionary action are ways of resisting the destruction of societies' ability to act upon themselves, or in other words the destruction of democracy, which begins with the loss of the social rights that were won with such difficulty in the course of that century. The same thinking informs the idea that only the state and voluntaristic policies can hold back the rising tide of neoliberalism.

Other analysts assert that, first, there is nothing inevitable about the triumph of markets and that political action is not powerless and, secondly, that it is not the action of the state, but the revival of social movements that will transform a situation in which we have certainly not been reduced to impotence.

We therefore have, on the one hand, an opposition which believes in globalization and its inevitability and which bears desperate witness against it by appealing to the republican state; on the other hand, we also have an opposition which rejects the view that transforming the economy and transforming society are two very different things, and which therefore does believe that there is still a field for political action, provided that our societies can avoid both the neoliberal illusion and the statist conservatism that is its mirror image.

The critique of the ideology of globalization put forward in the first chapter of this book shows me to be a supporter of the latter argument.

In all these cases, we can see the difference between the pessimists, who are calling for a desperate uprising inspired by anger and poverty, and those they call reformists because they refuse to say 'there's nothing we can do about it' and try to show that, on the contrary, it is possible to act, introduce reforms and construct new forms of social and political controls on the economy.

It seems that it is usually difficult for those who, like the *sans* (those without homes, jobs or papers), define their situation in purely negative terms, to become the nucleus of a social movement. And yet it is here, and especially among the *sans-papiers*, that we do find something resembling a social movement. There is, however, always the danger that the movement will become dominated by ideological or political vanguards.

The homeless

The housing crisis, like the unemployment crisis, has such general causes that it seems that only large-scale political and union action can do anything about it. Attempts to inititate such action have, however, been unsuccessful. In 1954, Abbé Pierre intervened directly in the housing problem by launching dramatic actions that were widely seen on television; the foundation of Droit au Logement ('The right to housing') in 1990 was an obvious reference to the winter of 1954. DAL organized the occupation of public buildings, won the sympathy of part of the population and obtained wide coverage in the media by involving celebrities and artists in its initiatives. Its action centred on the assertion of the right to housing, which was recognized by the 'Besson law' passed by the Rocard government. It was, however, difficult to bring pressure to bear on the authorities and to mobilize activists. After the successful establishment of the squat in the Rue Dragon and the transformation of the neighbouring Cours Désir into a space for solidarity, creativity and the exchange of knowledge, the split between the two factions became more pronounced and finally led to the split between DAL and the activists who founded Droits Devant! ('Rights ahead!').

The pressure of economic realities and of political and administrative interventions was so great that, despite the high profile it had at certain moments, the movement did not succeed in bringing any real pressure to bear on housing policy or in shaping new actors. It represented at best the starting point for the various *sans* movements, or in other words for protests against exclusion and poverty. These have a temporary influence on public opinion, but are never enough to create a movement. The main lesson to be learned from such actions is that it is very difficult to get beyond the phase of staging events for the media. Be that as it may, and even though the terms in which it was formulated were too general, the demand for the right to housing does show how a collective actor can begin to emerge.

The movement of the unemployed

There is nothing new about organizing the unemployed. During the interwar period in France, the Communist-inspired CGTU (Confédération Générale du Travail Unitaire) had many unemployed members (about 10 per cent) and a march for jobs from Lille to Paris succeeded in mobilizing 60,000 people at the height of the economic crisis of the 1930s. More recently, Maurice Pagat has tried to unionize the unemployed.

These precedents illustrate the central problem: the relationship between the action of the unemployed, and trade unionism. Left to its own devices, the unemployed movement oscillates between taking emergency action, sometimes violently and sometimes in a humanitarian way, and more general debates about reducing the working week or job-sharing.

The main organization – AC! (Agir ensemble contre le chômage! ('Act together against unemployment!')) – did from the outset have close links with the unions. At the same time, it remained broadly independent of its major partner, the CGT (Confédération Générale du Travail), which did itself take major initiatives. Both Claire Villiers, a member of the CFDT (Confédération Française du Travail Démocratique) who moved to the Sud-PTT (the postal workers' union in the south), and Christophe Aguiton, originally a member of the Ligue Communiste Révolutionnaire and now active in the same union, tried to combine autonomous actions, such as marches in France (1994) and then at the European level, with joint AC!–union initiatives, particularly in the Bouches du Rhône département. But AC! soon had violent disagreements with the unions, whose prime concern was to defend jobs. These became more pronounced when AC! claimed to be speaking on behalf of unemployed youths who had no future and who rejected the culture of work.

This led the movement to adopt a radically different discourse, especially during the 1995 election campaign. It now began to support the demands being put forward by every excluded category, including the homeless and the *sans-papiers*. This idea was an extension, in a more radical form, of the more general theme of the fight against *la fracture sociale* and for a new citizenship, which had been given a positive reception by the general public. That is why public opinion initially supported the occupation of ASSEDIC and ANPE offices at the end of 1997. But the government soon recovered the initiative, both by evacuating the occupied premises and by drafting an anti-exclusion law. A movement consisting of a few thousand unemployed and activists from very different backgrounds, and with very different attitudes and programmes, was powerless to resist this.

There were two very different aspects to this movement. First, it helped to give a new content to a demand-based action by advancing the notions of rights. What is more important is that it attempted to transform victims into actors and to demonstrate that the unemployed could, like the *beurs* before them, take organized action and make their voices heard, even though unionized workers did find it difficult to hear what they were saying. No movement has ever been faced with a more difficult situation for a new collective actor to emerge than this one was, and this is an index of its importance, but it also explains the weakness that led it to undertake purely media-oriented actions, as when it occupied the École Normale Supérieure at the invitation of some students. Such actions gave the movement a negative image. But while these turns off-course strengthened the government's position when it had the occupied offices evacuated, it should not be forgotten that this movement did make an innovatory contribution to the formation of new social actors and that it may resume its activity.

The movement of the *sans-papiers*

Whereas the homeless and jobless wore themselves out in protests against a situation that was difficult to transform because it called into question the economic organization of society, the movement of the *sans-papiers*, which could have been more marginal, transformed itself into a social movement. It did establish itself as an autonomous actor, and its adversary – the government – made it quite clear that that is what it was. It also enjoyed considerable public support, and at times the support of the majority because the defence of the rights of the few came to be associated with the de- fence of the rights of all, especially when Article 1 of the Debré law was interpreted by many as an attack on their personal freedoms.

The movement's strength and autonomy explain why it was never dominated by external interventions. The group of mediators merely tried to help people without papers with regularization where this had been refused or severely cur- tailed, but at no point did it try to lead the movement or define its meaning or impose a meaning on it. The movement established itself as a collective actor, mainly because it was based upon the earlier collective organization of the Malians who started it, and of the Chinese from Wenzhou who then took over from them. The Senegalese Ababacar Diop and Madjiguène Sissé finally became its main leaders and emblem- atic figures, and were interlocutors in the most important of the debates that took place within the movement.

After the occupation of the church of St Ambroise, the welcome given to the *sans-papiers* by Ariane Mnouchkine at the Cartoucherie theatre, and especially after the violent evic- tion of the hunger-strikers from the church of St Bernard, this movement was able to mobilize widespread support, which also fed on a more dynamic political emotion: fear of the Na- tional Front and an active rejection of its racist theses. The final outcome was that an autonomous action embarked on to defend the right of the *sans-papiers* to live normal lives in France was transformed into a broad movement which played an important role in political life, particularly after the pro- test demonstrations that took place when the National Front held its congress in Strasbourg.

The movement was not 'recuperated'. Although it had the support of far-left groups, humanitarian associations and celeb- rities, it never lost control over its actions and did not wear itself out in spectacular actions or staging events for the bene- fit of the media. It was not trying to reform society; its only objective is to regularize the situation of the *sans-papiers*. The very expression, which replaced 'illegal immigrants', indicated a desire for social integration that was not revolutionary but which did, given the migratory pressures generated by the international economic situation, provoke a fearful reaction on the part of the government and some sections of public opinion. In more concrete terms, it was the convergence of the *sans-papiers* movement and a citizens' rebellion against the Debré law that gave birth to actors who might otherwise have remained just as marginal as the homeless. They were therefore able to play a part in restructuring the social field and even in bringing down the right-wing government in the 1997 legislative elections.

The images broadcast by the media obviously helped the movement to expand, but it would be unfair to claim that the actions undertaken by the *sans-papiers* were primarily intended for the benefit of the media. The autonomous activity of those concerned and the invocation of the founding principles of the Republic were always the principal inspiration behind this collective action.

It might be objected that, as in the case of the *beurs*, a limited action was transformed into a political action because it received massive support from people for whom the struggle against the National Front and even the defence of their own personal rights was more important than solidarity with the *sans-papiers*. The objection is not acceptable because, while the *sans-papier* movement was transformed into a struggle against the Pasqua laws[5] and the Debré bill (which revealed, it should be recalled, the National Front's influence on the right-wing government of the day), and while it did, like any social movement, have political effects, the fact remains that its raison d'être was always the defence of very specific rights and the search for concrete solutions.

All the hunger strikes that punctuated this action confirmed that personal commitment was very important. All social movements encourage sacrifices and exemplary actions; in this case, the sacrifices were made in the name of the rights of individuals, and therefore had an ethical rather than a political orientation. And politics, which had for so long been bound up with the economy, was transformed when ethical demands entered the public sphere.

When actions are based on what people do not have (such as work, housing, papers, etc.) and not upon the recognition of a function or qualification, there is always a danger that the creation of social actors will become divorced from the political and ideological denunciation of an unfair order. In the social movements of the industrial era, these two components were linked together by the reference to the universalist principle of progress through reason. It is because there is no longer any such 'objective' principle, embodying an inherent philosophy of history, that we are now seeing a recourse to the idea of rights: the Rights of Man, as defined in 1789, but also, in more concrete terms, the right to work, housing and to live in security. We would now have to add cultural rights to the list. These rights are threatened by the Jacobin spirit when it rejects diversity and attempts to impose norms.

Now it is precisely the reference to the rights of the subject, and to the rights of minorities as well as those of the majority, that makes the new social movements so important. They represent a challenge to the dominant order, but what is more important, they also emancipate victims who are, at least in part, transformed into actors of social change. Conversely, there is a real danger, even a growing danger, that this 'affirmative' action will be taken over and manipulated by ideologies whose sole content is the denunciation of the dominant order and not the belief that new actors can emerge.

This subordination of social protest to political and ideological action no longer has the dynamic effect it had at the time when the communist parties lent their strength to working-class and anticolonial struggles, and at the same time used them to further their totalitarian political project. It is more reminiscent of the Latin American guerrilla campaigns of the last thirty years. These were in fact only indirectly related to the rural populations in whose name they took up arms, as their base was among young people from the radicalized urban middle classes, who regarded themselves as the vanguard that would liberate the people. This has led to some tragic impasses. The Soviet and Cuban models had to collapse before very different indigenous movements could develop in Latin America. Those models have been provided by Rigoberta Menchu in Guatemala, the Zapatistas and Sub-Commandante Marcos in Mexico, Bolivia's Katarists and the Indians of Equador. All these movements have rejected the politics of rupture, are based upon the assertion of a cultural identity and have adopted an actively democratic political line.

France has always been drawn to political extremism, and this has been detrimental to the formation of new social actors. This characteristic tendency is not a recent development and it is not confined to France. It is an avatar of the split between the Bolsheviks and their Menshevik adversaries, who dominated Russia's unions until 1913. In the 1970s, what I at the time called 'the new social movements' became exhausted precisely because they packaged themselves as 'Leninist'. New wine that is put into old bottles quickly turns to vinegar. This should not happen today: the *spirit* of May '68 (but not its political vocabulary) has been reborn and is stronger than ever. It has got rid of its old vocabulary and its archaic ways of thinking, especially in the action of the *sans-papiers* and that of Aides, which seem to be the most creative and emancipatory of contemporary protest movements.

Everyone understands that the demand for rights is a democratic demand, and that it is very different from the desire to 'seize power' or to make a complete break with institutions. It was the St Bernard collective and its supporters who blocked Debré's dangerous bill by invoking everyone's right to live in accordance with their own desires, needs and culture. There was never any question of taking power or starting a revolution.

To their credit, these movements have also reduced the gap between those who call themselves republicans and those who feel that they are primarily democrats. This is because recognition of cultural rights implies support for those institutions that can reconcile the unity of the nation with a diversity of interests, values and heritages. In France, as in the rest of the Western world and even further afield, we are losing confidence in both markets and communitarian politics. We are beginning to speak once more of the nation, citizenship, and of social and cultural rights. These terms are complementary and not contradictory. Citizenship can no longer mean fusing all identities into one unifying national consciousness, by repressive means if need be; it means greater diversity, more debates and more political representation within a collectivity whose main objective is to strengthen the rights of all rather than to subordinate everyone to an all-powerful and intolerant national unity and national interest.

These movements also reveal by contrast the decline of the voluntary sector, whose calls for solidarity and equality are, even when they are supported by sincere and generous volunteers, increasingly exploited by a state apparatus which is primarily interested in reducing its spending by entrusting some of its tasks to charity workers. The voluntary sector thus becomes an outpost of the administration, especially at the local level, and the administration is more concerned with vote-catching and gesture politics than in transforming victims into actors.

Cultural movements

Social movements capable of having an effect on the whole of social and political life will emerge only if a real link is established between the defence of victims and new cultural and social orientations. Such links are being established, and their formation is the most robust response to capitalist domination. We must analyse this in detail.

In the West, modernization took the form of the concentration of the means of action in the hands of an elite which was defined as rational and which asserted its leading role in the struggle against all supposedly irrational forces. Modernization was successful and it gave the West a supremacy that lasted for centuries, but the price that had to be paid was a general division of society, and the polarization of every domain: self-proclaimed rational entrepreneurs versus wage-earners who were supposedly lazy creatures of habit; colonizers who were bringing enlightenment versus 'savages' who were stultified by their rejection of progress; adults who were capable of self-control versus children who gave in to their instincts; rational men versus supposedly irrational women. The latter phenomenon found expression in the dominance of a masculine public life over a feminized private life.

We began to overcome these polarizations and oppositions between dominant and dominated long ago, and that tendency is now more pronounced than ever before. I have spoken elsewhere of the recomposition of the world.[6] The first manifestation of its recomposition was the labour movement: economic development is not reducible to authoritarian rationalization and the accumulation of resources; it requires the involvement of the majority in production, in consumption and in the management of modern society. We then saw colonial liberation movements rejecting a form of domination that was based not only upon force but also upon the haughty pride the colonizers took in their modernizing role.

In the second half of the twentieth century, two new major forces began to contribute to the recomposition of the world. The first was ecological thought and action which, rather than allowing human beings to dominate nature, made them the steward of a natural and cultural environment that was under threat and being impoverished by the power of technological and economic interventions on the part of societies that had been carried away by economic modernization. That this ecologism can, as Luc Ferry reminds us, take dangerously antihumanist forms, should not be allowed to conceal the reversal of perspective it has brought about.[7]

The women's movement is more important still, as the binary opposition between men and women has, in various forms, always dominated our cultures. Women began by demanding equal rights, an end to discrimination and control over their own bodies. In our countries, these demands were largely met at the legal level, but that did not automatically do away with real inequalities, as some had been too quick to claim it would. This was partly due to resistance on the part of the old hierarchical model, but it was also because the theme of equality carries with it a bias. It suggests to women that they should become equal to men and get access to the modes of life, the authority and the power enjoyed by men. And some of the failures of this egalitarianism stem from the fact that many women wanted a way of life that was different from that of those men who were most involved in the pursuit of profit and power. They attempted, in a word, to give a new content to women's identity. But this quest, like all identity-based movements, soon led them into a blind alley, and sometimes took the form of a self-marginalization which the most radical American lesbians – those in the queer movement – have done most to denounce. More recently, this has led to the formation of a more basic movement which is attacking the very principles of our polarized society, based as it is upon inequality.

The parity movement, which has had a considerable impact on public opinion and which has led to constitutional reform in France, is not the same thing as a policy of quotas, which seeks to re-establish fairness in a situation of inequality. It asserts that the 'man' of the Rights of Man exists only in the form of a man/woman duality and that the universality of rights – which must be defended at all costs – is inseparable from the recognition of the differences between men and women. Women wish to be both equal and different. This demand represents a challenge to the most basic component of the Western model of modernization: the production of the personality and of the future. We can no longer analyse the transformations that are taking place in our society without introducing the duality between male and female experiences. France is still a long way from doing so.

It should be added that a new front has now been opened up in the fight to bring about the recomposition of the world. We now speak of the rights of children and, quite apart from the spectacular scandals over paedophilia, we are hearing talk, both at school and at home, of the desire to give children greater autonomy and to enhance their ability to produce their own experience of life.

There is still a great distance between these great cultural movements and the actions that are being undertaken to defend the categories that are the most direct victims of our economic and social organization. These actions are much closer to the lived experience of those involved. And yet we know that, if they are to have any substance, social movements require that the defence of victims and the transformation of culture must converge. When they do so, the political scene can come back to life, whereas until very recently the attention of the majority turned away in disappointment from the confusion and turmoil it saw there.

One of the principal obstacles to the emergence of these movements is the intervention of people who do not believe in the possible existence of actors capable of defining positive goals. As we know, such people see in such movements only victims who are doomed to an inexorable fate and whose sufferings bear witness to the injustice of the social order. This ideology slows down the formation of social movements even when it does supply them with a discourse they cannot formulate for themselves. That is why it must be resisted.

It is difficult to establish links between negative and positive movements. The excluded – the *beurs*, the victims of discrimination, the homeless, the jobless and the *sans-papiers*, people with AIDS, the disabled and so many others – are primarily concerned with asserting their personal rights and at the same time fighting those apparatuses that govern and use to their own advantage the information society and a flexibility (or in other words job insecurity) that is presented as a precondition for competitiveness (and therefore growth).

The common feature of all these movements is that they collectively defend personal rights – the right to work and the right to a certain continuity of employment – as well as cultural rights. To say that such references to individual rights abolish any possibility of collective action is surprising in a country where the greatest text produced by the French Revolution is the Declaration of the Rights of Man, which is not only an appeal to the sovereignty of the people but also, and above all, to the defence of personal rights. To be more specific, what is new today is not the reference to freedom of opinion, freedom of association and freedom to organize: it is the invocation of the right to a personal identity, if by that we mean a unity that is constantly being constructed and transformed on the basis of a personal experience of life. That this 'ethical' defence implies collective actions is self-evident, and that is the meaning of many of the movements we can see today. We are, then, indeed talking about a political action and not a disembodied individualism that is indifferent to social relations and to relations of domination in particular.

Hence the importance of the *beur* movement of the 1980s and of the *sans-papiers* movement of the 1990s. These are the movements that did most to ensure the transition from defensive action to the assertion of rights, from protests against injustice to a reference to personal and collective attributes of which one can be proud (in the sense in which the labour movement spoke of a proud consciousness), no matter whether those attributes are professional, linguistic, ethical or religious. The homosexual movement, for its part, is not simply a struggle against discrimination: it also represents a 'gay' conception of the role of sexuality in social and personal life. While the purely defensive women's movement went into decline after its legislative victories and while the search for a female essence led only to marginalization, the action of women is, finally, an essential actor in the recomposition of the world, even if it does take the form of a trend of opinion rather than an organized political movement. Like the labour movement and the national liberation movements before it, the women's movement is a struggle to overcome the hierarchical oppositions between a rational, male, bourgeois and Western pole, and an irrational, female, popular and 'native' pole.

If it proves impossible to link these negative and positive movements, the former will rapidly be exhausted because of their internal divisions and the ease with which they can be manipulated by the authorities. In conclusion, how can we fail to see that, although these actions usually have only a limited lifespan and a limited capacity for mobilization, it is the formation of new social actors that is at work here? There is no guarantee that these struggles will merge or unite to form an equivalent to what we called the labour movement. But they are dealing with problems that are bound up with capitalist modernization and mass culture: they are therefore challenging the major forms of domination. That the government sees only their minority character is irrelevant. The important thing is not that they must be recognized by the state or by the dominant forces within society, but that they must make their mark on them and bring about profound transformations in the organization of society and the way we see society.

The recent (October 1998) *lycéen* movement clearly shows how traditional ideas about schools and education have changed. It is not the first such movement; *lycéens* have often supported student demonstrations with their restless presence. But this time, the tone has changed, perhaps because the movement's organization is so weak that the conventional discourses of classic union strategies have not immediately drowned out the voices of the *lycéens* – many of whom are in fact *lycéennes*. What they are challenging, quite apart from their material working conditions, which are in some cases unsatisfactory, is their place in the lycée. Our lycées perpetuate a truly academic culture and authority which may be acceptable to those who see them as leading to a predictable future, but which are unacceptable to those whose future is less certain and those whose personalities are at odds with a system that demands conformity to norms rather than the discovery of new ideas or modes of feeling. The *lycéens* want to be actively involved not only in the education they are receiving, but also in the changes that are occurring at every level from that of the law to that of individual schools. Because their demands are not strictly political, many observers find them too moderate. Those who wish to overthrow society are contrasted with those who want to play a greater part in it. This is a misunderstanding because these *lycéens* are not trying to impose a representation of society, but to tell us how they see themselves and their social environment. The development of autonomous personal projects, relations with friends from very different backgrounds, the desire for more direct communication with teachers, and an attachment to moral principles – the dignity and freedom of others – are more important than the classical analysis of schools as administrative and economic units. Their project is truly democratic because it is drawn up by those concerned, and because their discourse is free of external influences and reveals a depth of feeling that was previously hidden by talk, in the media and elsewhere, of young people being trapped in narcissism and their own particular culture. It is significant that many of these *lycéens* are capable of combining respect for their difference with an attachment to the French language, which is an indispensable instrument for communication and integration.

The spontaneity and poor organization of this movement rapidly reduced it to making quantitative demands that concealed its deeper meaning. but it has already achieved its main goal. In its support for the *lycéen* movement, public opinion has demonstrated that it had already begun to revise its traditional view of education. Education can no longer be based either on values such as knowledge, to which teachers must introduce their pupils, or on the norms of the school community itself. Education must be the servant of the creative freedom of the *lycéens* and must therefore take into consideration both their situation and their personalities. If it cannot do that, empty talk of equality can only increase inequalities at school.

Demands based upon personal projects rather than an objective critique of society have rarely been heard since 1968 – when they were heard in a very different context. This is indeed a social movement, as it is based upon personal self-assertion, and challenges the educational system and its rigidities in the name of a culture of discovery and innovation. Fifteen years ago I was already calling for and predicting the 'return of the actor'.[8] In the *lycéens'* demonstrations even when they are distorted by the provocations of the hooligan element, these are actors who are making their voices heard, with a combination of projects and criticisms, instead of their action being reduced to either a defence of corporatism or a total and ideological negativity that would destroy any real action.

Commentary

There are two possible responses to critics who demand our unconditional identification with social struggles (or at least those struggles that they themselves have chosen to support). Why, say the critics, attach such importance to these movements when some of them are weak and are led by political activists rather than by other categories, and when others are important only because they mobilize the liberal (rather than oppositional) defenders of rights that are guaranteed by the Republic? The real social problems lie elsewhere, and they have more to do with social disruption than protests. The real problems are corruption and speculation on the one hand, and antisocial behaviour on the other. We should really be worrying about the weakening of all social codes and the civic spirit.

But why confuse things that are so different, and, above all, why look at the life of society only in terms of order, legitimate as it may be, and not in terms of justice and the rights that are born of struggles, even when they are the struggles of the weak? The two kinds of public interventions that are required are in fact complementary. Acts of protest must be contained when they do not create a social movement and are purely negative; even stronger action should be taken against more militant forms of group behaviour if they have more serious consequences or break the law.

More attention should certainly be paid to measures designed to regenerate public life, but equal attention should be paid to the positive transformation of the self-destructive behaviour of victims into a capacity for positive collective action. The two goals have been pursued in parallel at times in the past, and they should be pursued in parallel today. For some, the main danger is the potential threat to the legal order; others are more worried about the threats to the social bond. Still others, myself included, emphasize the need for new social movements and new social actors. There are, however, no grounds for contrasting these three ways of struggling against a multifaceted crisis, provided that we do not allow ourselves to be seduced by the politics of fear, rejection and withdrawal. It is not only those who vote for the National Front who find a politics of that sort attractive.

4

The social left and the ultra-left

It was a difficult ordeal and one can understand why it made some people lose their heads. Unemployment went on rising and scatterbrained scribes told us day after day that national governments no longer had any influence on an economy that had been globalized, that nations were dissolving into markets, and that what had once been our society was now nothing more than an accelerated flow of largely unpredictable changes. A few ideologues began to sing the praises of the market deregulation that would set us free, while populists on the far right and the far left, together with a few politicians, screamed that the old country was heading for the rocks and that we had to get out of the new Europe before it was too late.

The fact of the matter is that the creation of a European currency does mean that we have to accept serious constraints, but it certainly does not condemn us to social regression or decline. Provided, that is, that we abandon the insane idea that we are impotent and actively defend ourselves against the financial storm, as it has national origins too.

Certain countries are allowing themselves to die of exhaustion. Others, like Japan and Korea, have made serious financial mistakes despite their great economic success. Still others, most of them in Europe, are gearing up for a new period of growth and at the same time fighting effectively against poverty and inequality. Certain countries are, like the United States, confident that their economic dynamism will make growing inequalities tolerable. These very different reactions demonstrate that politics is far from having no effect on the economy.

The first priority must be to put behind us the long period of confusion and panic that began in the mid-1970s, when both right and left, both the RPR (the Gaullist party) and the PS (Parti Socialiste) failed to see the changes that were taking place in the world economy. The policies adopted by the left in 1981 represented the height of irresponsibility and, since then, governments of both left and right have had to adopt realistic economic policies, but they have not always succeeded in convincing the majority of the nation, and perhaps not even themselves, that adapting to the globalized economy by no means makes it impossible to have a social welfare policy. Only Michel Rocard, who was able to take advantage of an improvement in the world economy, demonstrated that we could at the same time modernize the economy, introduce the RMI (Revenu Minimum d'Insertion or income support), bring about far-reaching changes in the tax system and even restore peace in New Caledonia, which, thanks to Bernard Pons' policies, was on the point of exploding.

For most of this period it seemed, in a word, that our only choice was one between a policy that would create unemployment, cut wages and destroy the social security system, and one of maintaining at all cost a state-managed economy that was leading us from deficit to corruption and poor management. Given that the past was impossible and the future was intolerable, how could the present be seen as anything other than a prelude to disaster? Given that politics seemed to be impossible, what else could we do but criticize and bay at the moon.

All it took for the climate to change was a new Prime Minister who could guarantee that the incompatible could be made compatible. We could both accept the fact that the economy had been globalized and that a greater European economic space was being created, and initiate major social projects. Common sense, intelligence and hope could come into their own once more. And a sporting victory confirmed that the French had recovered their self-confidence!

As usual, however, consciousness lagged behind experience: the hubbub in the distance was a reminder of the old fears. It indicated that we had lost confidence in political institutions, that we were unable to analyse situations and that we had jumped to the conclusion that there was no solution because we had not looked for and found the right way out of the neoliberal transition. And so France went on refusing to believe that new social policies could be drawn up in an open economy at a time when many European countries from Denmark and Holland to Portugal, Italy and even Great Britain had already adopted such policies.

This political and intellectual backwardness would not deserve great attention, were it not that it prevents us from really understanding today's demands, protests and revolts. It is not only that they are quite justified; the point is that they must give birth to the new social movements and the new political forces without which our political institutions will be unable to gain a new lease of life and without which our democracy will go on getting weaker. And so we see sections of the left speaking in the name of the Republic, but drifting closer to a right wing that is more interested in law and order than in fighting inequalities.

When political life loses its grip on social reality, extremist movements emerge to challenge a soft centrism. This disjunction has negative effects on both social struggles and political action. But when the political instrument that processes social demands is out of order, we have to accept that extremism is justifiable. The so-called French exception is to a large extent characterized by the political authorities' almost congenital inability to understand the social situation and to change it. Who would dream of criticizing the students of May '68 for expecting nothing from Pompidou's France? But today, the ultra-left no longer has any raison d'être, and we have to begin the essential task of making social protests and political action converge. When they are divorced, we are powerless to resist the follies of finance capitalism.

Today's task is to dispel the fog of populist interpretations and replace them with a serious analysis of the issues, choices and actors of the period we are now entering, and it is neither the period of *les trente glorieuses* nor that of the neoliberal transition that began in the mid-1970s.

The interpretation I am defending does not imply that we have to replace revolutionary slogans with an appeal to the good will of the government. It means that we must begin by seeing most popular movements as an expression of a will to emancipation and to win back the right to be an actor in the struggle against inequality and exclusion. The main point is, I repeat, that although globalization is supposedly beyond our control there is a will to act, even in the most unfavourable circumstances. It exists even when there is a very high level of unemployment, even though we have always been told that people who find themselves in that situation are condemned to impotence or to being manipulated by authoritarian demagogues.

The hunger strike in the reformed church in Batignolles undertaken by the *sans-papiers* who had come up against the government's refusal to regularize their situation, and by the anthropologist Emmanuel Terray, demonstrated the willingness to act for people who refused to see themselves simply as victims and saw themselves primarily as active protesters who were concerned about their own dignity and that of their fellows. For their part, the humanitarians who were critical of both their own action and the mistakes made by the charity business were as lucid as they were courageous, but they still reasserted their right to interfere in order to defend victims, and to show them as such in their suffering, in the violence that had been inflicted on them, in the denial of their dignity. In the same way, those who put people with AIDS on television and those who, like Jean-Paul Aron, let it be known that they had AIDS and did not have long to live,[1] helped public opinion to see them as human beings who were living through a tragic experience and who required compassionate treatment. Things were similar in the nineteenth century, when some people were content to denounce the destructive and degrading nature of industrial labour and working-class life, while others believed it was possible for the victims to become actors, thanks in particular to popular education and the establishment of trade unions.

As the domination to which they are subject becomes more impersonal and global, the theme of the powerlessness of the dominated becomes more widespread. Noisy interventions on the part of political and ideological vanguards make the idea of a social movement seem more and more illusory. And so the social movements die, suffocated by those who speak in their name. It seems that there is no room for anything between the ultra-left and the centre-right. The appearance of negative protests does, however, sometimes make it necessary to defend not only citizens or workers, but also human beings who have particular rights, particular experiences and a particular identity.

There is a growing discrepancy between discourses that denounce increasingly covert forms of domination, and discourses that resist the depersonalization induced by capitalism by appealing to the personal and positive experience of individuals and groups who are defined by a craft, a culture and a life history. Seen from the former perspective, the field of social struggles seems to be shrinking; seen from the latter, it seems to be constantly expanding. The economy is being globalized, but defensive movements are being globalized too as they appeal to lived experience and the desire to give it a meaning.

The difference between the two ways of interpreting popular movements and political interventions is, ultimately, a corollary of that between revolution and democracy. The basis for the revolutionary spirit is provided by the supposed powerlessness of actors, the central role attributed to the crisis, and the call for a vanguard leadership, while the democratic idea insists that all men and women must be regarded as potential actors who are capable of responsible actions despite the remoteness and strength of the dominant power.

But who believes in revolution today or still thinks it desirable? Almost no one, in countries where we enjoy freedom of political action, a few years after the collapse of the Soviet system. It is true that, in the dark days of the early 1990s, there was no longer any difference between right and left, and that the most monetarist policy ever to be adopted in France was introduced by Pierre Bérégovoy, a Prime Minister who was a member of the Socialist Party. The political situation has now changed, and tirades against *la pensée unique* have proved to be empty talk. At the same time, they increase the risk of antidemocratic action. The school of denunciation encourages extremism because extremism is able to cover up its lack of an analysis and its failure to understand the transformations that are taking place.

It is pointless to evoke the revolutionary/reformist dichotomy here: what matters is the difference between revolutionaries and democrats and, increasingly, that between those who believe in the possibility of action and those who do not, between those who subordinate society to the state and those who want to make social actors autonomous. The most extreme statism was preached, notably in 1995, when the defence of the public sector was elevated to the status of a democratic duty to resist the onslaughts of a civil society (and above all an economy) that was, it was claimed, governed solely by the pursuit of private profit. What a grotesque picture! The huge losses made by Crédit Lyonnais, the strike called by Air France's well-paid pilots, the SNCF's big deficit, even the failure of so many students to complete their first degrees and the bad management of many public sector companies, were all suddenly transformed into the crown jewels and popular victories! No one even thought to ask whether resistance to change and poor management in the public sector might not be making the economic crisis worse. Didn't the inflexibility of certain occupational situations and certain styles of management have something to do with the flexibility that was being forced on others? Were not the state's hold on the economy, and the continued strength of the administered economy also factors that made job creation and technological innovation more difficult?

Are we to conclude that we should leave the allocation of resources to the market? Certainly not. What we most need is neither more state nor more market, but less state and less market – we need more initiatives, more negotiations, more projects, and more truly social conflicts, through which the essential (and constantly changing) links will be established between the constraints and opportunities of the economy, and the demands or resistances of social actors. There are good reasons why the public is so harshly critical of the 'political class'. Neither parliament, the unions nor public debates seem to have played any decisive role in a history that has been reduced to the slow destruction of the administered economy by international competition and technological innovation. All social struggles, from the most defensive to the most innovative, are positive to the extent that they expand the political field, defined in the broadest sense as a public space. And one of the major obstacles to its expansion is the seemingly revolutionary, but in fact reactionary, call for more state intervention on the part of intellectuals who have become the watchdogs of the state petty bourgeoisie.

We should not let ourselves be deceived by the brief period we have just lived through. The movements to defend the public sector that punctuated it were obviously very important, and the protests associated with them will not fade away. But it is a mistake to think that populist ideologies captured their real meaning. The truth is quite the reverse.

As the countries of Europe emerge from the long neoliberal transition during which the economic and social systems of the postwar period were either destroyed or weakened, it becomes more obvious that new demands and new claims are being put forward. They can, however, be either backward-looking – and therefore no more than a form of resistance to economic and social developments that have to a large extent already taken place – or forward-looking. The formation or continued existence of an extreme left party favours the archaic solution. We can see this with Izquierda Unida in Spain and in a slightly different way in Italy, where Rifondazione Comunista brought down Romano Prodi's government, and in France, with the last disciples of Georges Marchais.

A second solution is to organize a far left which is social rather than political, but which still wishes to break with the system. The very noisy way in which this social ultra-left made its presence felt led many to believe it to be an expression of recent popular movements, whereas it provided no more than an ideological interpretation of movements that were still immature, even though they were rooted in a powerful collective experience. A left that attacks the left in this way will inevitably become part of an ultra-left political movement which will itself be very weak because, unlike in Spain, it will be made up of a multiplicity of tendencies and organizations ranging from the communists to the various Trotskyist groups and some of the Greens. To tell the truth, this outcome is very unlikely.

A third and very different solution consists in placing all our trust in a government of the plural left and prioritizing opposition to the right-wing parties that have proved incapable of resolving the crisis. This solution is no more acceptable than the other two. First, because while the socialist government did win the confidence of a large majority by asserting and demonstrating that economic competitiveness and social reforms were compatible, it did not listen to the movements initiated by the most excluded categories. There were, perhaps, electoral reasons for this, but the other reason is that the left's concept of the Republic leads it to behave just like the right in this particular domain. France, like its neighbours, is so divided by unemployment and job insecurity and is still so weak that one can quite understand the thinking of a government that is sensitive to the state of public opinion, and particularly sensitive to the opinion of the middle classes and those categories that are most threatened by demands put forward by the people who are suffering the worst effects of the crisis. Understanding does not, however, mean condoning. Thus, the one solution that is appropriate in the current situation has to emerge: social actors have to form, even if they are isolated and intermittent, because social actors alone are capable of bringing heavy pressure to bear on a left-wing government and at the same time supporting it strongly against a right which will, one day or another, succeed in recovering from its current decline. We should also be aware that it is because the right has been shattered that the left can now make a more vigorous critique of the government, and that *in years to come both social actors and political actors have a duty to come closer together so as to allow France to emerge completely from the neoliberal transition by reconstructing a social policy.*

What form will the social movements of the future take?

Certainly not that of the old labour movement, because social actors will recognize and insist on the necessary separation between political action and social movements, while still confirming the need for a link between the two. It is therefore impossible to believe that new social-democratic parties will be founded.

The immediate effect of the separation demanded between social action and political action is that social action cannot have any organizational unity, whereas political action does, by definition, have its organizational unity because what it is about is to prepare to take power. Social movements, in contrast, now act by organizing discontinuous *campaigns* that are so unrelated to one another that many are tempted to deny that there is *one* movement and to believe that we have an irreducible plurality of conflicts and issues. That is why the actors themselves, to say nothing of intellectuals, must demonstrate that these campaigns do have a common purpose and an underlying unity.

They are primarily campaigns against the state in so far as it serves the interests of the dominant economic forces. The social issue at stake in all these movements is individualism, which the dominant forces interpret as the freedom to buy in the market and which opposition movements define as self-determination and the assertion of the right of all individuals and all groups to singularity, provided that they recognize that everyone else has that same right.

The space that exists between organized social interventions and the decisions taken by the state has long been occupied by the political parties that act as mediators between citizens and states. The fact that the mediation does not always work well must not lead us to reject representative democracy. We would do better to accept that it is incapable of coming to terms with essentially social realities, and that organized social action usually takes place outside political institutions. Our definition of social movements is in itself an indication that they are by their very nature independent of political forces. In the past, the situation was very different; the only people to oppose the state were the notables and academics who spoke in the name of reason or even the people, but remained remote from the latter. There is no longer any basis for the double oligarchy of an authoritarian state and a learned elite, even though certain of the latter would like to keep their monopoly on speech and meaning.

The state now intervenes in every domain of both private and public life, and public opinion is no longer reducible to the judgement of a few interpreters; thanks in particular to opinion polls and the media, it now means the population as a whole. The media are neither neutral nor controlled by some ruling power. *Le Figaro* and *Libération*, or France 2 and Canal Plus are expressions of different ways of thinking. Research has, moreover, shown that, because they are usually simple, messages broadcast on television are received and interpreted in very different ways by different viewers, because everyone perceives the messages that are being broadcast in their own way.

When it comes to the media, three approaches are obviously wrong. The first is the claim that they present the 'facts' as 'objectively' as possible. This statement is inaccurate because the programmes we see on television – and the lectures given by a professor for that matter – do not simply report the facts; the discourse they carry is based upon choices.

This does not, however, mean that we can therefore say that the media express the collective opinion and interests of journalists, because their opinions are varied and so are their interests.

According to the third interpretation, the media serve only the interests of power; selective reporting and targeted entertainment eliminate the presence of real situations and real social actors, and decontextualize their message. Like the other two interpretations, this is a mixture of truth and falsehood. The space in which the media exist is in fact traversed by the same power relations, the same cultural trends and the same processes of professionalization (and even subject to the same academic tendencies) as any other form of public space. What makes it different today is not its nature, but its size. The *philosophes* of the eighteenth century, the political writers of the nineteenth, and the intellectuals and journalists of the twentieth century spread new ideas and sensibilities in creative ways; they also forced their modes of analysis and expression upon us and they surrendered to power and to the pressures brought to bear by certain sections of public opinion. Like political life in general, from parties to unions and the voluntary organizations of civil society, the space of the media is conflict-ridden. It also enjoys greater freedom at the level of cultural innovation than at that of political judgement in the real sense of that word. And while it is never reduced to simply speaking for the dominant forces, the space of the media is always subject to relations of domination.

Were it not for the media, there would be an even greater clash between an omnipresent state and an entire population that has been mobilized by accelerated social and cultural change. The lack of mutual understanding would be complete. When, as is the case in totalitarian countries, the media are completely in the hands of the ruling powers, private or public, they lose all credibility. When that situation does not prevail, they are the site for an unequal encounter between the public system and social life. And that encounter takes the form of an unequal confrontation between different ideas, opinions and interests.

General condemnations of the media can mean only one thing. They imply that the few have an absolute right to define the meaning of events and to inform public opinion, because they speak in the name of God, the nation or science. Such a backward step would be impossible without a high level of repression, as 'people' by no means think that they are totally manipulated and alienated, even though they are only too quick to complain about the poor quality or the objectionable content of the programmes they watch on television. As for social movements and those involved in other forms of struggle, they would be well advised to learn to use the media.

It is obviously easier to denounce so-called absolute domination in social life or in the media than to analyse real situations in order to decipher their various meanings and to define the role that might be played by independent social actors, and by protesters in particular. The important thing to note here, whether we are discussing the media or the social struggles themselves, is that we once more have to choose between an overpessimistic conception which sees the crushing effects of domination everywhere and refuses to accept that actors do have some autonomous space for action and expression, and a second overoptimistic conception which believes only in law and order and consigns anyone who does not conform to the outer darkness. The third conception, which I support, asserts that while the fields of the media and politics are never independent of the dominant social forces or state interventions, they are not devoid of autonomy and initiative. How can anyone who completely rejects this position believe in democracy?

Three lefts and a government

The end of the neo-liberal illusion has weakened and disoriented the right, which has been violently rejected by universal suffrage. The right is also paralysed by the National Front, as it cannot form a government with it and cannot form a government without it. Logically, the debate is therefore not so much one between right and left as a debate within the left. There are in fact two debates, and they define three lefts.

The most surprising debate is perhaps that between those who want to give a new priority to public order and to ensuring that institutions work properly, rather than to what they see as confused, directionless or dangerous social dynamics, and those who want, on the contrary, to prioritize social actors, their conflicts and their situation. The former call themselves *republicans*; their numbers are growing and they are bold enough to publish texts which might look to a casual reader as though they had been produced by the right, albeit a civilized right, whose prime concern is respect for law and order.

Their main strength comes, perhaps, from the increasingly shocking lack of realism of the *ultra-left*, the one which defines itself as the left of the left or as being to the left of the left. The latter description appears to me to be the more accurate, as 'left' is a political and not a social term and the defining feature of this ultra-left is its opposition to the government, which it accuses of having surrendered to *la pensée unique*. Many believe that only the ultra-left is talking realistically in a country that has been stricken by unemployment and job insecurity. It in fact mobilizes mainly to defend the public sector, and it is increasingly difficult to believe that a critique of poor state management necessarily leads to unfettered neoliberalism. The 'people' to which these intellectuals refer is in fact looking more and more like an ideological object.

Is there any living space left between the republicans and the populists of the ultra-left? The answer may be 'yes' in principle, but it is much more ambiguous at the level of practice. I have shown that today's *sans-papiers* and homosexuals have, like the *beurs* of the recent past and women and ecologists past and present, created cultural movements that defend both equality and difference and demand recognition of the cultural rights of minorities. We have to accept that there is a very real tendency for European governments to move to the centre-right or the centre-left. Those who say that 'the left' and 'the right' are two of a kind now sound so stupid! What gives them the right to regard as imbeciles all those who take a passionate interest in electoral battles between the left and the right? These governments are not only republican in the current sense of the word; they are committed to social reform, and greater European unity will take us closer to Jacques Delors's concept of a social Europe. But these are of course political rather than social actions. On the other hand, we are seeing manifestations of the ultra-left, at least in France. Even if one thinks, as I do, that these have misinterpreted the crises and protests we see in French society, they do exist. We have all met them, especially in the media. We therefore have to ask whether the increasingly centrist republicans and the ultra-leftists leave any room for anything other than a centre-left government?

I have just mentioned a certain number of social and cultural movements. It has to be admitted that they are fragmented, discontinuous and often dependent upon external supports. I therefore have to accept that the existence of this *social left*, which is demanding both equality and difference, is patchy rather than organized. Its importance is reflected by public opinion polls rather than by events. Although it has been marginalized by the government, it enjoys strong support among socialist politicians, in the CFDT and, above all, in many voluntary organizations. It is present in civil society, which now has almost no political voice of its own, rather than in either the large or small parties, or even the sects of the ultra-left. This book attempts to help it to both recognize itself and act.

The easiest way to understand the nature of the social left is to compare it with the ultra-left. The social left and the ultra-left are divided by a traditional conflict over ideas and actions. The ultra-left speaks of power and domination in terms that leave no room for autonomous action on the part of the victims. The only task of the 'proletarians' – old and new – is to burst asunder the contradictions of the dominant system. It is up to the political leaders and the intellectuals to tell the victims what domination means and to fight it by either relying on the state or taking control of the state. Such is the logic of revolutionary action.

The social left, in contrast, takes as its starting point the idea that all social movements begin with the active defence of a social reality and rights. Once, it was the nation against the king, and more recently, it was workers against bosses. Today, it is a matter of defending the cultural rights of all (and especially of minorities) against forced assimilation, irrespective of whether it is forced upon us by a market-dominated mass culture or by a communitarian power. Defensive actions and proposals for future action can be autonomous, and can therefore have a direct influence on political decisions. They do not simply denounce: they are born of hope, and are therefore democratically inspired.

In the type of society in which we now live, ten years after the collapse of the Soviet system and the Soviet empire, only tiny minorities support revolutionary thought. On the contrary, the extension of democracy from the political domain to social problems (which is slow and difficult) and now to cultural democracy (which still meets with strong resistance on the part of both left and right) now seems to be the central issue in public life. In that sense, it is very paradoxical to claim that only the ultra-left is paying attention to popular movements. While the ultra-left is preoccupied with defending the state economy against the globalization of the economy, it is in fact the other left that is trying both to defend those workers who are most in danger of unemployment and to have the cultural rights of minorities recognized. Reality will refute the relentless propaganda of those who would have us believe the opposite.

5

Two possible policies: the third way and a two-and-a-half policy

In the autumn of 1995, the increasingly ominous contradiction between social demands that were incompatible with the economic situation and an economic policy that seemed to be destroying the most legitimate social interests led to a fundamental crisis and a confrontation between a government that had no social policy and a public sector that was on the defensive. There appeared to be no solution. The support given by public opinion to a strike in which it took part 'by proxy' explained why economic goals and social demands seemed at that point to be incompatible. Hence the great demoralization that overcame French society, and hence too the obsessional idea of its inevitable decline: if we work towards a single European currency and if we are carried away by the globalization of the economy, we will soon see our wages falling, our social security system being dismantled, and unemployment and job insecurity spreading. All these threats were very real. They materialized with considerable force in Great Britain, and a good number of Germany's economic leaders regard them as positive developments. But accepting that these threats exist is one thing; reaching the pessimistic conclusion that we are trapped and unable to act at the national level of what is now an internationalized economy is quite another.

At the last moment, or just before we toppled into the void, we elected a government of the left which, from its first days in office, insisted that it was possible and even necessary to adopt both a neoliberal economic policy and a voluntaristic social policy. At the same time, the most naive admirers of the 'market society' found themselves alone in the face of the destructive effects of the financial crises that had erupted in various parts of the world and which were coming closer to the United States and Europe. For several years, the most active supporters of neoliberal policies, namely the World Bank and the International Monetary Fund, had been stressing in the pronouncement of their leading figures the universal need to reinforce the state's ability to intervene to deal with domestic upheavals and external threats that could not be spontaneously controlled by the market. In these conditions, it was clearly apparent that, while the old system of a state-controlled management of society had to be abandoned, it was not a neoliberal solution that was needed, but a redefinition of the state's role. We needed a state that could anticipate, mediate between and motivate the many different changes that our societies were experiencing.

It is clearly no longer a matter of trying to find a third way between neoliberalism and communism. Communism is dead and neoliberalism is collapsing under the weight of the international financial crises, even though it is still an important point of reference for everyone who distrusts state intervention. The intermediary ways that I propose to explore here lie, then, between this neoliberalism that is more voluntaristic than real, and a social democracy that has been crushed by the weight of state interventions and industries that have weakened the economy and benefited the state petty bourgeoisie.

Thanks to the influence of the sociologist Tony Giddens, the expression 'the third way' has become Tony Blair's watchword. It is now that of Chancellor Schröder too. The British Prime Minister even organized a meeting in New York between himself, Bill Clinton and Romano Prodi, but they could not, for different reasons, give him any real support. What is the Third Way? Essentially, it means replacing a welfare policy with an enterprise policy which presupposes both flexibility at the level of social organization and the empowerment of actors. This political conception is a response to the exhaustion of the welfare state, which slows down the collapse but cannot help the recovery, and might even make it more difficult. Job insecurity, which affects between 20 and 25 per cent of the population of the West, is fuelled both by French-style welfare and by British or American-style part-time work and short-term contracts. It is true that the weakest members of society still have to be given help but, according to the supporters of the third way, that can only be done by empowering them and doing away with the inflexibility that makes job creation so difficult. The good thing about the Blair policy, which also attaches great importance to improving state education and health policies, is that it reconciles economic and social goals. In the context of a post-Thatcherite Britain, where it is known as social-liberalism, this solution looks like a centre-left policy; it is in fact a form of neoliberalism tempered by social policies. It is open to criticism on the grounds that it merely empowers those who are already empowered, and helps those who are already 'in' rather than advancing the social integration of those who are 'out'.

Is there a third or intermediary way that does not take us back to the bad habits of the period when French politics was dominated by the defence of the interests of civil servants, public sector employees, the retired and everyone else who was dependent on public subsidies? If we have to reject both neoliberalism (solution 1) and the old social democracy (solution 2), is Tony Blair's third way (solution 3) all that remains? Looking to the history of European socialism for inspiration, I would like to suggest a two-and-a-half way which is midway between the old social democracy and the third way.

It differs from Tony Blair's project in that it prioritizes the use of economic means to bring about the social reintegration of the marginal and the excluded. In other words, it means giving increases in production and employment the priority they lost long ago due to monetary and financial problems. Do we have to remind ourselves that there is a close link between growth and employment? And should we not expect improved growth to come from factors other than the state of the international markets and the prevailing view? At the present moment, we have to increase domestic consumption and distribute purchasing power by cutting taxes and by at the same time supporting, in a voluntaristic way activities that create jobs, and asking the educational system to promote innovation. Just after the Second World War, the countries of Latin America, which had for a long time prioritized international markets, experienced a long period of 'interior' growth. Closing the frontiers is obviously no longer an option, but we do have to act upon the domestic factors that influence competitiveness and the solidity of a society that is now open to the outside world.

It is, for instance, unimaginable that development will occur in Latin America without a reduction in social inequalities and a struggle against the corruption and violence that blight the public administration and the police in particular. So far as France is concerned, we certainly have to overcome the corporatism of the state apparatus and its resistance to change, but we have to do just as much, if not more, to encourage those sectors that create jobs, to boost consumption and to ensure that education meets the needs of economic activity.

The Two-and-a-Half International, which was founded in Central Europe to provide an alternative to both Western social democracy and Soviet Bolshevism,[1] did not achieve a great deal, apart from launching a debate about the national question, but my allusion to it will help me to make myself better understood. While the third way can be defined as centre-right, the two-and-a-half way is an attempt to define a centre-left. The attempt to do so is all the more useful but difficult to the extent that France is still torn between a new social-democratic resistance to change and a politics of the left concerned to stimulate both output and redistribution. The latter is what I call the two-and-a-half way.

The distinction I am making between these two ways (the third way and the two-and-a-half way) or, to put it more simply, between the centre-right and the centre-left, may seem paradoxical. Having been thrown into turmoil by Mrs Thatcher's neoliberal policies, Great Britain could have swung further to the left, while France, which was still reluctant to embark upon the neoliberal transition, could have concentrated on getting rid of its outdated forms of state management. The opposite happened. Because of its role as the financial capital of Europe and because of the close alliance between London and New York, Great Britain has been drawn towards a pro-globalization policy, while France is still such a hostage to interest groups within the state that it cannot actively pursue a liberal policy.

Here we have the dividing line between the two ways. One gives priority to adapting the state to the market, and therefore to destroying what remains of the administered economy, but also to implementing educational and health policies that are related to an economic project; the other argues that an alliance between the state and social demands can resist the invasive power of the globalized economy. Could there be a better definition of the difference between the centre-right and the centre-left? Both solutions are of course still prone to serious illnesses: acceptance of inequality and social exclusion on the right, and being overprotective of categories linked to the state on the left. France must, I repeat, fight on two fronts: it is still reluctant to enter the neoliberal transition, but it is already time for the country to emerge from it. It is therefore true to say that France must adopt a policy that is at once centre-right and centre-left. But both the country's history and the lessons of recent years teach us that it must prioritize antiliberal interventions or, in other words, a centre-left policy, provided that these interventions always preserve the link between the goal of economic modernization and the objectives of social justice.

The important thing is to recognize that the economic and social policies of European countries are increasingly defined by the realistic choice they are making between these two strategies. The lazy-minded find it more agreeable to dream up choices that are as exciting as they are arbitrary, or even to denounce extreme neoliberalism in terms that are unrealistic in a country where the state still controls half of GNP, and to contrast it with a socialism that does not correspond to the policies of any self-proclaimed socialist government. We must not, then, confuse direct (and therefore justified) expressions of discontent with a serious analysis of a situation or realistic proposals for an alternative policy. Nor should we go on thinking that contemporary Europe, almost all of which is ruled by so-called centre-left governments, will necessarily remain at that end of the political spectrum. The new German government's rapid drift towards neoliberal theses is changing Europe's political complexion from centre-left to centre-right. France, where the majority of the electorate very often leans to the right, must rapidly prove its economic and social efficiency before the right recovers from a crisis that will not last for ever and before left-wing voters become disillusioned with a policy that is too prudent or even timid.

It is with this in mind that I now outline the three priorities that appear to me to define the two-and-a-half policy.

Prioritizing work

In the area of social policy, the first priority must be to reprioritize jobs. The central objective must be to reconcile greater flexibility on the part of industry with a defence of labour, which must not be seen solely as a commodity. If we are to halt the rise of ideologies that view labour flexibility as a precondition for economic success, we must draw up a labour policy that is compatible with the new conditions of economic life, the speed of technological change and the opening up of national markets to a world in which there are more and more industrial countries and in which, more importantly, an unbridled finance capitalism is increasingly divorced from economic life. It is certainly not easy to define and apply such an employment and labour policy, but recognizing that as our absolute priority is in itself an important step in the right direction.

An obvious comparison comes to mind. It has at last been recognized that we have to lower the cost of the least skilled labour without cutting wages that are already low. Michel Rocard's introduction of the Contribution Sociale Généralisée has cut employers' social security contributions by broadening the tax base and levying taxes on all forms of income and not just wages. While there are disagreements as to how such changes should be introduced, no one denies that industry alone cannot solve the problem of unemployment, especially in big industries where jobs are inevitably being shed as labour productivity rises. In the same way, the massive and rapid shift away from traditional industrial jobs towards other sectors can no longer take the form of the channelling, as Albert Sauvy used to say, of the labour force from the secondary to the tertiary sector in the same way that workers were diverted from the primary to the secondary sector after the war.

This transformation of work must be organized. Major resources must be allocated to training people for new activities that usually require a higher level of general knowledge, and there must be far-reaching changes in the educational system. We must also prioritize the defence of work and, in addition to providing help for both the unemployed and industry, train the active population for the new forms of production and commerce. The most pessimistic will say that this in fact means creating more unskilled jobs in the tertiary sector, or what the Americans call 'McJobs'. Such jobs do indeed exist, and France must create many more of them in retailing and particularly in the hotel, catering and personal services sector. These sectors are, however, creating fewer jobs than those created by new technologies – these are what the Americans call 'Microsoft jobs' – and than those that will need to be created to guard against the major risks that threaten our societies.

Only the latter category of jobs will be taken into consideration here. Does anyone believe that an advanced technological society can function with manual labourers? On the contrary, the general level of skills and education is rising rapidly.

As social policies are redirected towards job creation, wages must come to represent a greater proportion of GNP. Their share has fallen considerably in recent decades. As we can see from the continued rise of share values, which is still real despite the severity of the crisis, and the success of financial investments in the strict sense of the word, this has been to the advantage of mobile capital rather than industry and productive investment. As Jean Boissonnat points out, the implementation of an active employment policy is not a matter for the state alone; it must also be implemented by cities, regions and the professions, as well as the voluntary sector, with its activities ranging from humanitarian action to the improvement and protection of the environment.

I find it difficult to understand those who talk of the end of work. If they are trying to do away with a productivist ideology that subordinates every aspect of life to productive activity, they are right. Industrial society was not, however, a work-based society; it was, rather, a society based upon production and profit. We now tend to think of work as having a positive value, not only because of the destructive effects of unemployment on both the personality and social life, but also because the proportion of interesting and skilled jobs is constantly rising. This is not an argument against cutting the length of the working week, particularly for those in unskilled jobs. First, because the division of labour is based upon the idea that labour does have a value, and secondly because the long-term tendency for the working week to become shorter has been greatly slowed down over the last fifteen years. During that period, rising productivity benefited capital rather than labour. We have to cease believing that we have made the transition from a work-based society to a consumer or leisure-based society.

A policy such as this can succeed only if it based upon a social agreement. Without the agreement of the trade unions, Denmark and the Netherlands could not have implemented a policy that has allowed them to reduce unemployment without damaging their social welfare systems. If French trade unions were as strong and well-informed as Italy's, many apparently insurmountable obstacles could be swept aside.

The weakness of French trade unionism, together with divisions between the unions – and they are growing rather than diminishing – is one of the main reasons why French society is so bad at seizing the initiative. Neoliberal economic policy has not weakened the unions in all countries. In Sweden, Germany and Italy, the unions are strong enough to help shape economic and social policy. This is not the case in the United

States or Great Britain, and nor, for different reaons, is it the case in Spain or France. In France, the unions are unable to play a major role because they are critical of everything, tend to describe the situation in doomladen terms and speak the language of rupture. Reducing the pressure brought to bear by employers is essential if we are to see the revival of unionism we need, but it is more important still to look, like the CFDT, at the internal preconditions for the reconstruction of union action, especially in the competitive sector, where it is now almost non-existent.

Sustainable development

Employment policy must also be based on a major change that Michel Aglietta defines thus: the priority given to increasing labour productivity must give way to finding ways of making capital more productive. It takes a great deal of capital to create a job in traditional industries; much less is required in both the knowledge industries – research, innovation and education – and personal services. We are still trapped by the industrial model that tries to create big industries with high labour productivity, backed by the big banks and managed with the agreement of the unions within the framework of major projects drawn up by a voluntaristic state. It is time to give a new priority to innovation, education and solidarity.

Above all, we must change our conception of economic growth. In its earliest stages, modernization means the accumulation of labour and capital, which ensures high levels of growth. The base of growth then has to be broadened, and it has to be recognized that this requires a high level of education, efficient means of communication and an adequate public administration. This gives us endogenous or self-regulating growth. We have now entered the third stage of what the Brundtland Commission and the Rio Conference call sustainable growth. Sustainable growth is impossible without risk protection against major ecological, nuclear, medical, social or cultural threats. We have to rebuild our cities, reduce unemployment, facilitate intercultural relations and avoid the marginalization of the old and the young. Many think that the most important sectors of economic life should be so managed as to satisfy the requirements of the international markets, but this is not the case. As America's success demonstrates, growth depends primarily upon innovation. It also requires capital to be invested in production rather than in international financial circuits; domestic consumption must rise and the country's internal social and political equilibrium must be respected or improved. It really is high time that our economic activity gave a new priority to technological innovation and social problems, not only for reasons of social justice, but because innovation and solidarity are the basic elements of sustainable economic growth.

Those who believe in the inevitable triumph of *la pensée unique* ignore the realities of a European Union that is broadly committed to social-liberalism or centre-left policies which, in very different ways, stress the need to reconcile a liberal economic policy with measures promoting social solidarity. There is no contradiction between defending those categories that suffer the worst violence and outlining a new economic policy. On the contrary, the two things are complementary. The real obstacles to an active social policy are, on the one hand, protesters who adopt a purely negative stance and, on the other hand, governments which remain indifferent or hostile to movements that support the disadvantaged in the same way that the French government was indifferent to the movement of the *sans-papiers*.

From this point of view, it is obviously vital to put an end to the weakening of political management in both Europe, the United States and Japan. The state itself is weak. Political parties are in a state of decay and are no longer seen as representative. They sometimes give one the impression of having been transformed into mere electoral machines. Japan has gone much further than other countries in the weakening and discrediting of political parties. How can they now be reconstructed? Primarily by reformulating the terms of the underlying debate, or in other words restructuring the right/left opposition. Its main expression today is: should we prioritize competitiveness and therefore economic flexibility, and accept that 20 per cent of the population will have to be left by the wayside, or should economic policy also be a policy of social integration that fights exclusion? The right and the left have very different positions on this question, even though the ultra-left sometimes finds it difficult to see that this is the case. The right relies on an economic logic, and the left on a political logic. So much so that in Europe the crisis in political management is a concern for the left rather than the right. The crisis sometimes takes the extreme form of corruption, and sometimes that of the absence of any real social programme. In other cases, it takes the form of an inability to get beyond minor readjustments that in fact do nothing to change economic policy. The result is the emergence of opposition movements, and sometimes violent movements, and the growing importance of 'civil society', or in other words of a new type of political action that is both less organized and less continuous than that of parties and unions. In their different ways, both the United States and France provide good examples of the vitality of civil society, which flourishes as political parties and trade unions become weaker. The strength of their union federations has so far protected Germany and Italy from this parapolitics which, while it is innovatory in some respects, also reduces the ability to think and act on the part of parties that are sometimes difficult to describe as being on the left.

Our capacity for political decision-making has, then, been weakened in two ways, and it must be strengthened in two ways. On the one hand, there must, as almost all governments realize, be more state intervention in the economy; on the other, unions and parties must recover their ability to represent popular categories. The convergence of the requirements of a mobilized economy and increasingly fragmented social demands will lead directly to greater political intervention. On the other hand, and this is where my focus lies, there is an obvious need for stronger and more lucid new social movements if we are to enhance our society's ability to choose its own destiny.

Intercultural communication

For much more deep-lying reasons, French society has the greatest difficulty in challenging the self-image that has identified it with universal values to such a degree that acquiring French citizenship and becoming integrated into a society governed by reason and the state seemed to be the best (or even the only) way of defending its values. This tradition has obviously been reinforced by a justified horror of totalitarian regimes, and especially regimes that claim to have an ethnic, national or religious basis.

This French Jacobinism is, however, as pernicious and unrealistic as the authoritarian communitarianism that rejects all social diversity. I am not trying to defend cultural differentialism or an identity politics that denies the possibility of all intercultural communication. I am trying to resolve the central problem of the Rights of Man. Can we preserve the universality of the Rights of Man and at the same time ground them in the reality of particular social and cultural situations? Did we have the right, a hundred years ago, to speak of the right to work, and of laws and conventions that applied to particular social categories defined primarily by a specific type of relations and position within the system of social domination? Didn't this infringe the civil rights that had been granted to all? It now seems obvious to us that the response to this question has to be positive. And yet many nineteenth-century republicans were opposed to workers' rights because it seemed to them that they were essentially less universal than the civil rights that had been won by the French Revolution.

Similarly, in a society where mass culture is triumphant, where information technologies influence both culture and our personalities, and where migrants are increasingly producing cultural hybrids, we must win cultural rights for all in the same way that we won social rights for all. This is not simply a matter of tolerance, and it is in fact difficult to see how a dialogue between cultures can take place in the absence of universal channels of communication. It is, rather, a matter of bringing about what I have termed the recomposition of the world, or in other words reintegrating into culture and social life social and cultural categories that have been 'invented' as inferior. If we see immigrants only as people who have been driven out of their backward societies by poverty and who simply want to adopt a Western way of life, we are creating major problems for ourselves. What happens if they are not assimilated, either because of unemployment or job insecurity and the xenophobia of the 'host society'? It is essential to reconcile equality of opportunity with a recognition of the cultural personality of immigrants. They do need work, but very often they also need places of worship and the opportunity to negotiate the transition from one cultural field to another. The increasingly common refusal to recognize cultural diversity is becoming the basis for what has to be called a nationalist right, even when it claims to be on the left.

If we are to communicate, we have to be different but we also have to speak the same language. That is why the idea of minorities has become so important. A minority wishes to be recognized as being different, but it also democratically recognizes majority rule. Institutions must protect and further everyone's attempt to establish their singularity; they must respect cultural rights or, as Amartya Sen would put it, ensure that it is possible for the greatest possible number to be as involved as possible in those activities to which they ascribe a positive value. Provided, of course, that they recognize that others have the rights they are demanding for themselves.

We must stop thinking that individuals are there to serve society, and are defined by their functions and the contributions they make to collective life. Individuation must be the central goal of education at home and at school, and it must also be promoted by the law. This process is already well under way. It will then be possible to 'recompose' every individual, that is, to reconcile within the individual modern reason and all the things it has rejected and inferiorized. Psychoanalysis has been the main explorer in this domain, and many contemporary currents of opinion are attempting to rehabilitate it. The effort must not, however, be allowed to degenerate into some vague 'New Age' spiritualism. The movement of the *sans-papiers* was also, and above all, a movement of self-affirmation on the part of Malians, Senegalese and Chinese, and what we call the suburbs (*banlieues*) have seen the emergence of movements defending Arab, Algerian, Moroccan and Kabyle identities which are at once heritages, creations and ways of becoming part of French society.

Why reduce these collective actions to the struggle against exclusion and arbitrary power, when they are also struggles for self-recognition? Why reduce the homosexual struggle to a struggle against discrimination, when it is also an assertion of a homosexual personality and an attempt to modify the role of sexuality in both personal, interpersonal and collective life?

Talk of the multicultural society is almost meaningless because the expression does nothing to shed light on the preconditions for communication between cultures. Our objective must be intercultural communication, or in other words a recognition by all of the right of all to recombine, each in our own way, involvement in the world of technologies and the economy with the reinterpretation or defence of a culture. No collective action can have an emancipatory effect at the national and/or international level unless it is part of this demand for cultural rights.

Europe and the nation

Given that the major technological and economic forces tend increasingly to operate at a supranational level, should the political field, and in much more general terms the expanded public space, be established at the European level or even at world level? There are good reasons for arguing that it should, and Jacques Delors is right to defend the idea of a political Europe, and to suggest that the election of the European Parliament should take place at a truly European level rather than being held at the national level.

Without wishing to dismiss these efforts and these hopes, it is, however, possible to imagine a very different development. We are witnessing the end of the close correspondence beween all the registers of collective life – the economic, the social, the political and the cultural – that were once unified within the framework of the nation. Increasingly, aspects of economic life are developing at a supranational level; at the same time and at the oppposite extreme, cultural identities, old and new, are proliferating. These are sometimes located at a supranational level, but usually exist below the national level. We might therefore conclude that political institutions could best operate at an intermediary level, whether that of the nation, the region or the city.

The idea of the nation is thus being divorced from that of the nation-state, just as the idea of the nation-state was divorced from that of the constitutional state, which originally referred to the establishment of absolute monarchies or oligarchical political societies and not to the idea of the sovereignty of the people which provided the basis for the idea of the nation-state, especially after the French and American revolutions. The idea of the nation must, however, rid itself of its quasi-religious connotations and come to designate the common space in which intercultural communication, solidarity and modernization can both function and be defended. Public opinion is closer to this conception of our national existence than to the ideologies that insist on thinking that France has a monopoly on universalism and modernity.

The nation is becoming increasingly important because sustainable development usually involves an increase in activities that are not directly profitable, as is the case with education, health care and the protection of the environment. It is true that in France the state has too great a share in public spending (54 per cent as opposed to 50 per cent in the European Union, and 40 per cent in other Western countries). But the need to reform the state and to cut public spending must not become an obstacle to increased spending on health, education and the protection of the environment, though it has to be acknowledged that this non-commercial sector will to a growing extent be controlled by regions or cities, professions or voluntary organizations, and that the state's role will decline.

A country is defined by the manner in which it manages its resources and the way it resolves its domestic problems, rather than simply by its position in the international markets. The Scandinavians realized this long ago, which is why they have a high level of national consciousness. The same must happen in France, where a 'Louis XIV' conception of the state, which is as pathological as it is influential, seems to be forcing the French to make the radical choice between State and Market, even though both options are absurd.

Can one be French?

Everything I have written here can be seen as a salvo against the French 'headquarters', and against the continued attachment of many of my fellow citizens, and especially those who run institutions, to the cult of the dominant state which both guides and punishes society because it regards itself as the agent of reason and progress. It is true that I have opened fire on the HQ, but I can both justify and modify my attitude.

The justification for my criticisms is the fact that the French model is in ruins, or exists only in school textbooks and the sermons of state philosophers. It is not some economic or technological failure that has caused us such problems over the last twenty years; it is the increasingly obvious discrepancy between official France's centuries-old discourse about itself and reality, between republican discourse and the continued existence of social inequalities – some of them created by state intervention – between the France that welcomes exiles and the France that closes its frontiers to, for example, Bosnian refugees, and between the eulogies to the modernizing state and the follies of the Crédit Lyonnais and other public sector companies. France is making no more mistakes than neighbouring countries, but no other country's self-image is so out of step with its practices. So much so that it seems to many both at home and abroad to be a country that is blinded by pride and paralysed by its foundation myths, and which makes progress only when forced to do so by external forces. France is obviously not reducible to this outdated republican-progressive discourse. I am not, however, speaking here of landscapes, literature, vineyards or technology. I am speaking of the ideology in whose name France is governed, in which it is becoming bogged down. The high price we are paying for this is being borne mainly by the weakest.

I do think it necessary to condemn the French model, but this is not to suggest that we have to accept the extreme neoliberalism of the 'market society', to which, as I have said, I am categorically opposed. To do so would be absurd, especially at a time when the illusion of the globalized society is being dispelled. We are beginning to see the real face of finance capitalism, and we need state intervention against it. The French model is a model for management and power rather than regulation; but regulation, foresight and a desire for justice are precisely what we need. My criticisms are therefore not directed against the 'obstacles' that stand in the way of the free movement of the markets, but against the way that the old model for the management of society blocks the search for new modes of regulation that are efficient in economic terms and fair in social terms.

Conclusions

The role of intellectuals

In an ideal social movement that was both 'conscious and organized', as in a completely democratic and enlightened political system, the role of intellectuals would be minor or non-existent. The same would be true if, conversely, social change were under the exclusive control of one economic interest, one political will, or of routine and bureaucratic corporatism. It is when there is no effective principle that can unify social and political life that the intellectuals intervene. They originally did so to condemn political or religious powers that forced arbitrary or scandalous decisions on society. At a later stage, as more and more social actors appeared and as democracy was extended, intellectuals intervened in social conflicts and debates so as to bring out their meanings because the actors could not be fully self-conscious in situations of crisis or dependency and because those meanings were hidden by the ideologies imposed by the ruling classes or the parties that spoke in the name of the people, the nation or the masses. The Dreyfus affair marked the turning point between these two eras, and it therefore became a central reference for the study of 'intellectuals'. It was, it will be recalled, at this time that they were first called by that name.

There are of course different kinds of intellectual. The most classic, and perhaps also the most visible, is the accuser, all of whose attention is concentrated on the critique of the ruling system. He reveals the interests that are concealed behind the moralizing discourses, and speaks of the sufferings of those who are exploited, alienated and manipulated. Everything that has been said in this book indicates how important these intellectuals are in contemporary France. Hence the importance of Pierre Bourdieu, who is the exemplary representative of this type of intellectual. These intellectuals dominate much of the press, and not only *Le Monde diplomatique*. This image of the intellectual was most visible during France's last colonial wars. Jean-Paul Sartre and his associates, and especially Frantz Fanon and Jean Genet, were intellectuals who were defined by their critical and negative role rather than by their interpretation of how power was being resisted. And during the period 1965–1975, Louis Althusser was a guide for many intellectuals. It was, however, Michel Foucault who most successfully combined critical thinking and work of great intellectual quality.

The second type of intellectual, unlike the first, identifies with particular struggles or particular oppositional forces and becomes their organic intellectual or even their ideologue. The lasting power of the Communist Party in France afforded many intellectuals the satisfaction of being the stars of public meetings or, if they were more honest, of having the feeling that they were disinterested participants in emancipatory movements that were building a better future. The collapse of communist ideology and power has obviously been a major blow to this type of intellectual, all the more so in that many of them were irresponsible enough to let themselves be persuaded to defend China's barbarous cultural revolution. It would, however, be as unfair to condemn this type of intellectual out of hand as it would be to suggest that they no longer exist. Many of the intellectuals who signed petitions, and took part in marches, demonstrations and even hunger strikes, marked in a perfectly honest way their solidarity with demands and protests that are being ignored by the public authorities. Their role is limited in that they play no part in defining the meaning of the action in question and simply bear witness, but it is also an important role in that it is an expression of the will of intellectuals who could easily be absorbed into the establishment, and who are, in a sense, part of it, to go on acting in solidarity with the most deprived categories and those who are least able to find their own voice.

Going beyond these two categories of intellectuals, it should also be noted that more complex figures appear in more difficult situations. First, we have those intellectuals who do their job, which is to analyse and understand, by looking for the meaning of the actions, which they may either support or oppose. They position themselves in relation to real actors whose action, like any historical event, has several different meanings at once, and try to define those meanings and to elucidate what they see as the primary meaning. They can, however, be described as intellectuals – as opposed to experts or professionals – only if what they say and write is intended to serve as a critique of social power or, more directly, as a protest and an oppositional force.

The difference between these intellectuals and those in the first category is that those I am talking about here believe in the existence of conscious and effective actors, even though they recognize their limitations, whereas those in the first category believe only in the critique of the internal contradictions of crises and evil. This does not mean that intellectuals who attempt to understand actors and to give an interpretation of their actions are optimists, or that they believe that good will always triumph over evil. It simply means that they do not believe that the triumph of evil is inevitable or that there is nothing more to history than internal crises and the hegemonic strategies of the dominant forces.

Once we believe in the possibility of action and inventiveness on the part of the dominated, we are in a position to distinguish between what is good and what is bad about the actors' analyses or strategies. These intellectuals are in a difficult position: they believe in the actors but keep their distance from them because they mount a critique of their actions and discourses, and struggle against the justificatory ideologies that are generated by all social and political action. Activists, however, much prefer intellectuals who denounce the crimes of their adversaries to those who analyse *their* action, even when they do so in sympathetic terms.

France has known many intellectuals of the third kind, even if they have often combined an abrasive and creative critique with an attachment to outdated social and political references. Many of them came from the communist left, from Socialisme ou Barbarie or from the Union des Étudiants Communistes. Many leading figures such as Cornelius Castoriadis, Claude Lefort, Jean-François Lyotard and François Châtelet belonged to and were products of these groups. The most emblematic figure of this type of intellectual is still, however, a man from another generation, André Malraux, because his political interventions were both real and directly transposed into his books.

These intellectuals can intervene only in a democratic society, as their critical task consists mainly in deciding which aspects of a given demand can be handled by institutions, which are non-negotiable and which have been contaminated by outside interests or ideologies. It must of course be made quite clear that they intervene because they recognize in the action they are studying either ethical or social issues that go beyond political intervention. These intellectuals, and it seems to me that they play the most important role, are never politicians because they see in social action a non-political principle that cannot be fully recognized by the political system. It is easy to mock those who speak of the defence of rights and equality, but defending them is the usual reason why intellectuals make interventions. They try to determine, in a given political situation, what can be handled by institutional mechanisms, what is the product of the rational pursuit of personal or collective self-interest, and what invokes values that transcend any social organization. Being opposed to all unifying visions, no matter whether they are moralizing or display an unbounded trust in political, juridical or educational institutions, these intellectuals destroy these false unities and attempt to identify the issue most at stake in collective action.

There is also, finally, a fourth category of intellectuals. They can be described as utopians in the positive sense of the term, in that they identify with the new trends in society, personal life or culture and make them more visible, without blinding themselves to the social conflicts that arise over the social management of these transformations. Edgar Morin is the most creative utopian in France, but he remains interested in the interpretation of social movements, especially when they are young and still poorly organized.

There has much been talk of 'the end of the intellectuals'. The expression is meaningless. Max Gallo spoke more accurately of the 'silence of the intellectuals' in the early 1980s, but he did so for the wrong reasons.[1] The vast majority of French intellectuals refused to live in Mitterrand's court, and those who did join it do not have happy memories of that episode. Their silence was very meaningful, as we saw at the beginning of Mitterrand's reign, when a number of very different intellectuals supported Edmond Maire's CFDT not only to defend Solidarity and the Polish liberation movement, but also to pass critical judgement on the new President's policy.

In more recent years, the most conspicuous trend was that associated with the collapse of communism and the rebirth of the democratic idea. This task had been already undertaken by Raymond Aron before the 'new philosophers' assumed it. Then came the years of the great demoralization and of the decay of political action. During this period, we heard both those who denounced the dominant order and the analyses of the 'interpreter-intellectuals'. I regard myself as one of the second category. The difference between the two was symbolized by the disagreements over two petitions in the early autumn of 1995.

All these families of intellectuals can coexist, and it is in fact their coexistence that makes up the consistency of intellectual debate, and of intellectuals themselves, as they spend at least as much time fighting one another as they do analysing real historical situations. This general conclusion is especially valid in the present situation in that our societies have no unity, do not conform to any hegemonic logic and are increasingly fragmented. We can therefore see new forms of action and thought taking shape whose emergence has to be uncovered, but at the same time, the exclusion zones drawn by accusatory intellectuals are also expanding. Between the two, the attempts that are being made to reorganize the political system are keeping the intellectuals well away.

The only family of intellectuals that is in decline today is that of the ideologues who have organic links with a political organization. So much so that it is beginning to look like an endangered species. This is both natural and desirable, as this type of intellectual refuses to recognize that others also have their place and because philosophies of history and faith in the 'Party' of the future are in terminal decline.

We are, on the other hand, seeing the reappearance of every other type of intellectual. Indeed, many people are already complaining about the deafening noise of their quarrels. This is not, however, a return to the past. The explanation for the relative silence of recent decades is that a historical period is coming to a close, while the return of the intellectuals is associated with the replacement of the analysis of systems by the interpretation of actors. Their return therefore relates to the revival of the democratic spirit, the recomposition of struggles and above all the defence of the basic rights of freedom, equality and solidarity.

From rejection to intervention

More so than any other society in Western Europe, French society has long refused to analyse the way the world is being transformed and to discover new policies that can channel, use or curb the social effects of the economic changes that are throwing the world into turmoil. It has tried to perpetuate the social and political model which was adopted by most countries after the war, and which gave the state a central role in national reconstruction and modernization.

This model has been inexorably weakened, both in France and elsewhere, partly because it produced an administered economy that is becoming less and less efficient, and partly because the globalization of the economy and the speed of technological innovation require an ability to adapt and to develop initiatives that the French management model does nothing to encourage. In the 1980s, the very low rate of growth led to a big rise in unemployment. Although the economic situation was deteriorating, France wanted to continue along the path of social progress: longer holidays, earlier retirement and an uncontrolled rise in spending on health. All of which presupposed a high rate of growth. In May 1981, France gave an enthusiastic reception to the measures taken by François Mitterrand, who had just been elected President of the Republic. Less than two years later, a disappointed France accepted a policy reversal that was pursued as incoherently as the earlier policy. At the beginning of the 1990s, we then saw the left adopting a very strict monetarism and sacrificing everything to the strong franc. Although Michel Rocard successfully implemented both economic and social reforms, France experienced a series of failures after his departure from office. Every Prime Minister promised to reconcile economic realism with social progress, and they all failed in the attempt. Public opinion had believed them, but then withdrew its support. Faced with the imminent introduction of the single currency, Jacques Chirac finally encouraged Alain Juppé to adopt a policy of public spending cuts. This made serious inroads on people's income, and led to a new rise in unemployment. The major crisis that erupted at the end of 1995 was neither the product of a social movement with a vision of the future nor simply the effect of resistance on the part of those with vested interests to defend; it signalled the collapse of a political society that simply could not bring about the economic transformations needed to bring down unemployment and at the same time keep the social welfare system intact. The suicidal belief that economic openness was incompatible with social integration took France to the edge of the abyss.

It is not difficult to understand the popularity of all the references to *la pensée unique*: politics *seemed*, to left and right alike, to mean submitting to the demands of the international markets and working towards a monetary union whose only goal was to facilitate the movement of capital.

The history of France over the last twenty years has been mainly the history of the decay of its political system, and it has been hastened by the attacks of judges who, as in Italy or the United States, set themselves up as judicial powers by revealing the illegal methods that were being used to fund political parties. The executive was impotent. A parliament with no real powers was voting through laws in an empty chamber, and judges were acquiring an independence that was as worrying as it was necessary. How, in these conditions, could initiatives that were beyond the control of political institutions fail to make their presence felt? Those categories that were most worried about economic openness and Europe voted for the National Front, which was using immigrants as scapegoats and overstating the level of crime in the *banlieues*. As it grew stronger (and won up to 15 per cent of the vote), the National Front destroyed the unity of the right. On the left, the abstention rate rose and the Communist Party continued to collapse. A general mood of discontent led public opinion to support every big strike as a way of expressing its loss of confidence in both the government and the country's future.

The crisis in our political institutions aside, the main reason for our long-term impotence is the decomposition of social actors and of relations between them. Employers are on the defensive because so many companies are now trading in an international market. The trade unions are tying themselves in knots in their attempt to defend the public sector. Political ideologies insist on believing that nationalizations are an essential precondition for social progress or, conversely, that opening up the economy will automatically settle social problems. The social struggles that have animated the last twenty years developed outside this aging world. They mobilized the most underprivileged categories: *beurs* affected by xenophobia, people with AIDS who had been victimized by a deplorable administrative management system, immigrants with no papers who had been trapped into an impossible situation by absurd laws or brutally sent back to their own countries, homeless families, and the unemployed. They also developed against a backdrop of social decomposition and growing job insecurity (which now affects between 20 per cent and 25 per cent of the population), violence and antisocial behaviour in many *banlieues*. Because they were responses to negatively defined situations and because they were born of despair, these struggles were primarily manifestations of rejectionism on a

grand scale, and they were supported by an increasingly an-
guished public opinion. Public opinion was quite right to support them, as they expressed a will to action, and the
population of France could see that its floundering governments had no such will.

The struggles of the excluded were also characterized by
uncertainty. While they did express and reveal suffering, they
usually did not succeed in drawing up an alternative policy or
in putting forward proposals, and this usually condemned them
to being cannon fodder for political vanguards or intellectuals
who put words into their mouths. And yet these movements
were not always just manifestations of a crisis: to varying degrees, they did allow new social actors to emerge; they did
organize individual victims into conscious groups that were
prepared to act. Which of these two tendencies will become
dominant?

The former seems to be more pronounced. Like every other
aspect of public life, these movements have become caught up
in the logic of the crisis they helped to reveal (and to exacerbate). They look to the state for a solution in the belief that it
is as free to act as it was in 1945, and perhaps in the expecta-
tion that it will create a new Popular Front. In 1995 in particular, this did seem to be the dominant tendency. Denunciations
replaced analysis and proposals, just as rupture with the system replaced negotiation, and just as rejectionism replaced initiatives. We have already entered a new phase. Just as the logic
of denunciation and crisis was, in material terms, dominant
during the years of advanced political decay we experienced
between 1991 and 1997, so it is now becoming possible to
regain a certain confidence in our ability to both act and invent
a new political discourse, and to formulate new issues, new
conflicts and new institutional ways of dealing with them. It is
becoming possible, or even absolutely necessary, to take this
path. It is to this that this book is intended contribute.

Epilogue

This book is not a pamphlet. I have nothing against pamphlets; they are necessary (and dangerous) but they are not to be confused with either reflections or attempts at analysis, or even with expressions of personal opinion. Pamphlets are defined by what they are against. In the fight against the enemy, they mobilize whatever comes to hand: proven arguments, unconfirmed journalistic reports, witticisms, personal attacks and so on. A good pamphlet does not tell lies, but it does keep quiet about everything that does not serve its purpose. It is pointless to criticize firefighters for using dirty water to put out the fire. Pamphlets can take many different forms: reports from international organizations, speeches by political leaders and investigative journalism are all pamphlets, even though they are not polemical in tone. Conversely, *J'Accuse* is not a pamphlet. It is a detailed analysis of the facts and when you close this text you do not say that you agree with Zola's ideas, but that you have been convinced by his argument. The title of this book is sufficient indication that my goal here is not to begin a polemic.

But while this book is not a pamphlet, it is not as neutral as a book by a doctor, a teacher or a jurist. My prejudice is the belief that people make and think their own history by fighting both the material domination they suffer, and the way their behaviour is explained in the name of material logics that are supposedly superior to all forms of social action. In my view, what we have to understand are social relations, actions and rules. And I make common cause with the writers, economists and sociologists who are involved in the same project.

The criterion whereby we should judge books and articles devoted to social or personal life is, it seems to me, as follows: do they or do they not help actors to arrive at a better understanding of their actions, and their causes, meaning and effects? If an explanation or an interpetation, which may well have its intrinsic qualities, deceives social actors or encourages them to act irrationally or emotionally, it cannot be correct because its objective is not to describe 'facts' but to understand actors, and therefore to reduce the distance that always separates an action from the actors' representation of that action.

This is a difficult task to accomplish. All actors like to be admired, flattered and held up as examples. But when actors identify with their analysis, they almost always make mistakes and therefore become weaker.

This statement applies to all historical moments, past, present and future. We must keep our analytic distance, or even establish it. We must look critically at events so as to decipher the multiple meanings they contain. At the same time, we must be motivated by the sympathy that encourages us to discover a project where others see only disorder. What working in this way loses in immediate approval or popularity it gains in usefulness, if we accept that the work done on itself by a society or a social movement (as by an individual on their personal life) is slow, difficult, punctuated by crises and characterized by zones of obscurity. If I did not admit that there is a price to be paid for this work of elucidation, I would be contradicting my own definition of social knowledge. We should be proud of the fact that there is a price to be paid. Especially at a time like this, when the explanations are so slow in coming and when arbitrary discourses, which in scientific terms could not be more false, are invading the field of knowledge, but when we can already see the way out of these misunderstandings.

We must resolutely reject all discourses that try to convince us that we are powerless. How long can we go on listening to and speaking a language that contradicts what we feel and even what we do? How long are they going to go on telling us that we are subject to the absolute domination of the international economy, when we invent and defend ideals, discuss reforms and break the silence every day of our lives?

Is it so difficult to understand the difference between those who talk only of domination and those who believe in the possibility of emancipation? Between those who speak of rejection and those who understand hope? The French spent the nineteenth century failing to understand anything about the emerging labour movement and applying to it categories specific to the history of the French Revolution. Let us not begin the new millennium by continuing to confine new struggles and new hopes within discourses that are one society behind our lived experience.

Notes

Introduction

1   Literally 'the one way of thinking' or 'the only way of thinking', *la pensée unique* is roughly equivalent to the TINA ('There Is No Alternative') of the Thatcher years in Britain.

1   The return of capitalism

1   Alain Touraine, *The Post-industrial Society. Tomorrow's Social History: Class, Conflict and Culture in the Programmed Society*, trans. Leonard Fox Mayhew (New York: Random House, 1971; original French edn, 1969).

2   Four exits

1   Concerning a Renault car plant in Belgium. The announcement in February 1997 of its imminent closure sparked a 'Eurostrike' involving both French and German workers. Unlike Peugeot, Renault is in the public sector.
2   The 'black hussars' were the militantly secular schoolteachers (especially at primary level) who helped create the modern educational system after the separation of church and state in 1905.
3   Founded by Daniel Defert in 1984, Aides is the French equivalent of the British Terence Higgins Trust, giving medical and social support to sufferers from AIDS.
4   The 'Debré law' of 1996 further restricted immigration and abolished the ten-year resident's permit introduced in 1983. Article 1 required those who had foreign nationals living with them to obtain registration certificates from the police.

5 Viviane Forrester, *The Economic Horror* (Cambridge: Polity, 1999).
6 Popular term for the government formed by Lionel Jospin in June 1997; representatives of the Communist Party, the Radical Socialist Party and the Greens agreed to cooperate with the Socialist majority.

3 New social movements?

1 *Beurs* is popular term for the French-born children of early generations of North African immigrants.
2 See Françoise Gaspard and Farhad Khosrokhavar, *Le Foulard et la République* (Paris: La Découverte, 1995).
3 See Frédéric Martel, *Le Rose et le noir: les homosexuels en France depuis 1968* (Paris: Seuil, 1996).
4 Introduced by legislation adopted in 1998, the PACS provides a legal framework for both heterosexual and gay couples who are cohabiting.
5 Laws drafted by the Minister of the Interior in June 1993, and designed to further restrict immigration by reducing the number of family reunions. The stated purpose of the Pasqua laws was to reduce immigration to zero.
6 See Alain Touraine, *What Is Democracy?*, trans. David Macey (Boulder, Col.: Westview Press, 1997).
7 Luc Ferry, *The New Ecological Order*, trans. Carol Volk (Chicago: University of Chicago Press, 1995).
8 Alain Touraine, *Le Retour de l'acteur* (Paris: Fayard, 1984).

4 The social left and the ultra-left

1 See Jean-Paul Aron, 'Mon SIDA', *Le Nouvel Observateur*, 30 October 1987.

5 Two possible policies

1 Founded in Vienna in 1921, the 'Two-and-a-Half International' was officially known as the International Working Union of Socialist Parties and was meant to provide an alternative to both the Second (Socialist) International and the Third (Communist) International or Comintern.

Conclusions

1 Max Gallo, 'Les Intellectuels, la politique et la modernité', *Le Monde*, 26 July 1983.

Index

AC! 60
Act Up 36, 54–5
affirmative action 29, 64
Aglietta, Michel 97
Aguiton, Christophe 60
Aides 36, 54, 55, 65, 118n3
AIDS 36, 54–6, 77, 113
Althusser, Louis 107
Amsterdam treaty 12, 16
Aron, Jean-Paul 77
Aron, Raymond 110
assimilation 29, 101

banlieues 113
Bérégovoy, Pierre 78–9
beurs 48, 51–4, 70, 113, 119n1
black hussars 32, 118n2
Blair, Tony 24, 90–1
Boissonnat, Jean 96
Bourdieu, Pierre 27, 107
Brazil 24
Britain 3, 10, 24, 89, 90–1, 91, 92–3
bureaucracy 22–3

capital controls 14–15
capital/labour 14, 96, 97
capitalism 3, 5, 9, 11–12, 14–15, 20–1, 24, 57–8
car industry 26, 118n1
Cardoso, Fernando Henrique 24
Castel, Robert 37–8
Castells, Manuel 13
Castoriadis, Cornelius 109
centrist politics 7, 23, 86, 92–4, 98
CFDT 87, 97, 110
Châtelet, François 109
children's rights 68
Chile 14
China 14, 24
Chirac, Jacques 112
citizenship 26–7, 38, 65–6, 100
civil rights 100

civil service unions 25
civil society 26, 87, 99
civil unrest 36–7, 50, 52, 62, 65, 73, 76
Cohen, Élie 16
Cohn-Bendit, Daniel 36
collective action 4, 6, 19, 50; beurs 51–4;
cultural rights 102; globalization 5, 19;
homeless 59; homosexuals 54–5;
immigration 102; sans movements 57,
70, 102; social movements 9, 19, 48–9;
victims 73
colonization 67
communism 10, 110
Communist Party 107, 113
communitarianism 51, 100
Confédération Générale du Travail Unitaire
60
la contre-pensée unique 1, 23
Contribution Sociale Généralisée 94–5
corruption 15, 99
crime 113
cultural identity 18–19, 25, 52, 53, 64–5,
100–3
cultural movements 66–73, 86–7
cultural rights 2, 28, 53–4; collective
action 102; homosexuals 55; immigration
52, 64, 101; republicanism 30; social
movements 51, 86–7; social rights 47

Debré law 37, 62, 63, 65, 118–19n4
Defert, Daniel 54, 118n3
Delorme, Christian 52
Delors, Jacques 41, 86, 102
democracy 3, 21, 41, 78–9, 87–8
Denmark 96
development modes 10, 20
Djadja, Toumi 52
domestic consumption 92, 98
domination 3, 33–4, 36, 67, 78, 108,
115–16
Droit au Logement 59
Droits Devant! 59

dualization of society 25, 28

École Normale Supérieure 39, 61
ecologism 67
economics: globalization 10–11, 13, 18–19;
  politics 8, 11, 75; social movements 3;
  social policies 81–2, 90, 91, 93, 105
education: black hussars 32, 118n2; child-
  centred 32–3; headscarf affair 52–3;
  individuals 101; innovation 92, 97; *lycéen*
  movement 71–2; republicanism 28–9;
  social actors 77; social inequality 31–2,
  39, 40; state 46; teachers' movement 39
egalitarianism 4–5, 10, 28–9
Elias, Norbert 2
employment 46, 94–5, 96, 97; *see also* job
  insecurity
empowerment 90–1, 108
European Parliament 102
European Union 39–40, 41, 42, 74, 86, 89,
  98, 102–4
exceptionalism 11, 30, 76
exclusion 2, 11, 37–8, 91–2; domination 34;
  globalization 39; social actors 114; social
  movement 7, 69

Fanon, Frantz 34, 107
Ferry, Luc 67
financial crisis 15–16, 90
Forrester, Viviane 38
Foucault, Michel 107
France 10; bureaucracy 22–3; civil service
  unions 25; economic/social goals 22,
  43–4; exceptionalism 11, 30, 76;
  globalization 43–4; immigration 51–4;
  neoliberalism 20–1, 93; political action 2,
  4, 65; self-image 104–5
Front Homosexuel d'Action Révolutionnaire
  54
fundamentalism 18

Gallo, Max 110
Gaspard, Françoise 53
Genet, Jean 107
Germany 89, 96, 99
Giddens, Tony 90
globalism 41
globalization 2, 4, 16–17, 89; capitalism 5,
  24; collective action 5, 19; cultural
  identity 18–19, 25; domination 33–4;
  economics 10–11, 13, 18–19; exclusion
  39; France 43–4; inevitability 57–8;
  nation-states 6; social actors 19
Groux, Guy 46

headscarf affair 52–3
Hegel, G. W. F. 33
Hilferding, Rudolf 14
homeless 38–9, 58–9
homosexuals 36, 54–6, 70, 102
hunger strikes 57, 62, 63–4, 77

identity politics 18, 51

immigration: assimilation 29, 101; collective
  action 102; cultural identity 52, 53,
  100–1; cultural rights 52, 64, 101; France
  51–4; National Front 63, 113; *see also*
  Debré law; Pasqua laws
individual rights 63–4, 69–70, 101–2
individualism 82
Indonesia 14, 15
industrial democracy 3, 21
industrial society 8–9, 50–1, 96
information society 8–9, 13
innovation 40–1, 92, 97, 98
institutions 1–3, 21–2, 41, 76, 113
intellectuals 3, 6–7, 40, 80, 83–4, 106–11
International Monetary Fund 90
interventionism 19
Islam 52–3
Italy 96, 99

Japan 10, 15, 74, 98
job insecurity 81, 86, 91, 113–14
Jospin, Lionel 43–4, 53
judges 112–13
Juppé, Alain 112

Khosrokhavar, Farhad 53
knowledge industries 97
Korea 10, 15, 74
Krivine, Alain 37
Krugman, Paul 14

labour: capital 14, 96, 97; retirement age
  29; working conditions 29, 47–8, 96
labour movement 26, 31, 34, 49, 67, 117
labour policy 94–5
Latin America 64–5, 92
Lefort, Claude 109
left-wing politics 35–6, 38, 80–1, 85–7,
  92–4, 98; *see also* socialism
lycéen movement 71–2
Lyotard, Jean-François 109

Maastricht treaty 12, 16
Maire, Edmond 110
Malraux, André 109
market forces 9–10, 11, 74, 90
Martel, Frédéric 54
Marx, Karl 27
May '68 uprising 36–7, 65, 76
media 83–4
Meirieu, Philippe 31–2, 32
Mexico 14
Mitterrand, François 52, 110, 112
modernization 9–10, 20, 25–6, 66–7, 97
monetarist policies 78–9, 112
Morins, Edgar 110

nation-states 6, 9, 10, 14–15, 102–4
National Front 21, 35, 39, 52–3, 63, 85,
  113
nationalisms 12, 34, 49, 67
neoliberalism: financial crisis 24, 90; France
  20–1, 93; nation-states 14–15; social

policies 18, 91; trade unions 96–7;
  unemployment 17
Netherlands 96

occupation of buildings 39, 57, 61, 62

Pacte Civile de Solidarité 55, 56, 119n4
Pagat, Maurice 38–9, 60
pamphlets 115
Paris Commune 27
parity movement 68
Parti Socialiste 75
Pasqua laws 63, 119n5
la pensée unique 1, 6, 17, 23, 29, 30, 79, 98,
  112, 118n1
polarization of society 66–7
political action 2, 4, 65
political rights 26–7
politics 3, 99, 112–13; economics 8, 11, 75;
  extremism 17, 79, 80; social actors
  79–80; social movements 82–3, 99; *see
  also* centrist politics; left-wing politics;
  republicanism; right-wing politics
Pons, Bernard 75
populisms 20, 21, 35–6, 38–9, 42, 77, 86
productivity 95, 97
proletariat 31, 86–7
public sector 11, 48, 79, 104, 113
public spending 103–4, 112

Rawls, John 29
Reich, Robert 13
republicanism 2, 26, 28–30, 42, 85–6
retirement age 29
retirement pensions 16, 46
Revenu Minimum d'Insertion 75
revolution 3, 78–9, 87–8
right-wing politics 39, 85
Rights of Man 53–4, 64, 68, 69–70, 100
Rocard, Michel 75, 94–5, 112
RPR (Gaullists) 75
Russia 15–16

les sans-papiers 48, 61–6, 113; collective
  action 70, 102; Debré law 37; hunger
  strikes 57, 62, 63–4, 77
Sartre, Jean-Paul 107
Sauvy, Albert 95
Scandinavia 104
Sen, Amartya 101
social actors 1–2, 5, 85; domination 36,
  115–16; education 77; empowerment
  90–1, 108; exclusion 114; globalization
  19; homosexuals 36, 54–6, 102;
  intellectuals 3, 6–7, 40, 80, 106; politics
  79–80; populism 42, 77; republicanism
  2, 42; social movement 48–9, 73; state
  28; trade unions 77; victims 3–4, 6, 77;
  worldism 42

social inequality 31–2, 39, 40, 104–5
social justice 4–5, 10
social-liberalism 91, 98
social movements 34–5, 38, 116; collective
  action 9, 19, 48–9; cultural rights 51,
  86–7; economics 3; exclusion 7, 69;
  individualism 82; media 84; politics
  82–3, 99; public sector services 48; *les
  sans-papiers* 61–2; social actors 48–9, 73;
  social rights 51; strikes 45–6;
  unemployed 48, 60–1; victims 69
social policies 18, 75, 81–2, 90, 91, 93, 105
social problems 30–1, 89, 111–14
social rights 26–7, 34, 47, 51, 87
social welfare 16, 18, 81
socialism 9, 78–9, 81, 112; *see also* left-wing
  politics
SOS-Racisme 52, 53
state 9–10, 26, 28, 46, 98–9; *see also* nation-
  states
state interventionism 5, 27, 83–4, 90, 99
statism 79
Stiglitz, Joseph 14
strikes 26, 45–6, 48, 118n1
student–worker movement 36–7, 65, 76
sustainable growth 20, 97–9
Sweden 96

teachers' movement 39
technocrats 10
technology 40–1
Terray, Emmanuel 77
third way 90–1, 92–3
totalitarianism 12, 33–4, 51, 84
trade unions 17–18, 46, 49, 60, 77, 96–7,
  113
transnational companies 13
truck-drivers' movement 47–8
Two-and-a-Half International 92–3,
  119–20n1
two-and-a-half policy 93–5

unemployment: neoliberalism 17;
  occupation of buildings 57; populisms
  38–9; social movements 48, 60–1; state
  27, 74, 81, 86, 96, 111–12; trade unions
  60
United States 12, 13, 16, 18, 75, 98

victims 3–4, 6, 69, 73, 77
Villiers, Claire 60
voluntarism 40, 66, 92

wages policy 95–6
welfare state 3, 10
women's movement 30, 49, 67–8, 70
working conditions 29, 47–8, 96
World Bank 90
worldism 41, 42